Jacky Newcomb is author of *An Angel Treasury* and one of the UK's leading angel experts, giving talks and workshops all over the UK. She runs her own column as mystical agony aunt 'Dear Angel Lady' for the UK's CHAT *It's Fate* magazine and also writes regularly for magazines such as *Woman's Own*, *Fate & Fortune* and *Vision*. She writes regularly about angels, spirit guides and after-life communication, and receives letters to her website (www.angellady.co.uk) from all over the world. Jacky has made many TV appearances including ITV's *This Morning* and LIVINGtv's *Psychic Live*.

Other Books by Jacky Newcomb:

An Angel Treasury

For more information please visit:

www.JackyNewcomb.co.uk – Jacky's main site

www.GabrielMedia.co.uk – Where to find Jacky's schedule of appearances and workshops

www.AngelLady.co.uk – Jacky's main angel website

www.AfterLifeCommunication.co.uk – Jacky's After Life Communication links and articles

Jacky Newcomb

'THE ANGEL LADY'

a little angel love

Spread happiness and inspiration,
with help from the angels

HarperElement
An Imprint of HarperCollins*Publishers*
77–85 Fulham Palace Road,
Hammersmith, London W6 8JB

The website address is: www.thorsonselement.com

and *HarperElement* are trademarks of
HarperCollins*Publishers* Ltd

First published by HarperElement in 2005

3 5 7 9 10 8 6 4

A catalogue record of this book is
available from the British Library

ISBN-13: 978 0 00 720570 7
ISBN-10: 0 00 720570 8

Printed and bound in Great Britain by
Martins the Printers Ltd, Berwick upon Tweed

contents

acknowledgements

To my loving family and friends – all of them. Thank you for your support and being who you are, especially John, Charlotte and Georgina. I am proud of you all.

Thank you to every person who has shared their own knowledge and experience with me. Each personal angel experience is a piece of the 'great puzzle of life'.

preface

After my first book, *An Angel Treasury*, I was inundated with requests for another book. I receive hundreds of letters from all over the world. 'We love your book. Can you make a smaller version which we can carry around?' So here it is. At first I wondered if I could ever write anything more about angels. I honestly felt I had written everything there was to write about angels but in fact that wasn't true at all – there is still so much more and the task will never be complete of course!

Your lovely angel stories just poured in and I am grateful to each and every person who was kind enough to share their stories with me here. Angel stories form the beating heart of the book and people love to read them. They bring inspiration and comfort.

Since I wrote *An Angel Treasury* I have realized how fascinated people are with the idea of having their own guardian angels. I have given many radio and TV interviews and published lots of magazine articles on the subject. Many of the questions were repeated over and over, so I have tried to address these new questions here. As you can imagine in this line of work, each query I had myself was answered by my own angels in either 'coincidental meetings', coming across the information in a book 'accidentally', or the perfect story coming to me at the right time! But you and I know that this was so much more than coincidence. I asked my angels to help me, as I always do.

If you are reading this book right now then you have probably been sent by your own angels … a coincidence? I doubt it! Now is the time to begin to explore angels in your own life. If you are a new reader then welcome. If you have read my work previously then welcome back.

In the last year I have been working on many projects including an angel DVD and several guided angel meditation CDs. Lots more things are in the 'pipeline'. Each person will find their own way of working with their angels and this book and other ideas presented to you will offer suggestions for ways which feel right for you. I don't believe there is any 'one way' to do this right!

I love to read your own personal angel experiences and look forward to hearing from you. You can find me at my website: www.JackyNewcomb.co.uk or post letters via the publisher at: Jacky Newcomb (author), c/o HarperCollins.

Jacky Newcomb BSYA (Psy.D)

guardian angels –
beautiful beings of light

'Angels belong to a uniquely different dimension
of creation which we, limited to the natural order,
can scarcely comprehend.'

BILLY GRAHAM

Who are these beautiful beings of light? Is it true that we each
have our own guardian angel watching over us? For as long as
recorded text has existed, people have written their stories of
personal protection by some unseen presence, a being of light.
And before recorded text? Stories were told around the camp

fire of these celestial beings, and passed from generation to generation.

The shepherds in the Bible were frightened of them; others revered them. Many saw angels as unapproachable. Most religions recognize angelic messengers in one form or another and many people believe in guardian angels, our own special defenders.

> 'An angel of the Lord appeared to them, and the glory of
> the Lord shone around them, and they were terrified. But
> the angel said to them, "Do not be afraid. I bring you
> good news of great joy that will be for all the people."'
>
> LUKE 2:10–12

Never more than today have we been able to share these stories without ridicule. The appearance of an angel, an angel visitation, is called 'angelophany'. But not all experiences are related to actually seeing angels. All angel experiences, in whichever way the angels choose to draw close, are precious gifts which grow with the sharing. Each time a story is passed on the experience expands, and lifts and enlightens more and more people. Just the telling of angel stories is a powerful thing in itself!

People from all over the world have shared their angel stories with me. Each story is individual to the owner, although there are many similar themes which run through these special moments. People who have never met have experiences, maybe years apart, where the essence or reflection of their story is the same … the touch on the shoulder, the time in their life when it happens, the vision of a 'being of light', and so on.

> *'An angel is an intelligent essence, always in motion.*
> *It has free will, is incorporeal, serves God, and has*
> *been bestowed with immortality. Only the Creator*
> *understands its true nature.'*
>
> JOHN OF DAMASCUS

Do you have a story of your own, or one that a close family member has confided? Often we forget and then the tale of another will make us go, 'Oh yes, that reminds me of something which once happened ...' Other people say, 'I have never told anyone this before,' or worse, 'I told someone once and they said I must be dreaming so I never shared it with anyone again ... until now!' Isn't it sad that one person might feel the need to take a life-changing moment away from another? In most cases there are no witnesses, it's not something which is easily proven, but why worry? I have never felt the need to prove any of my experiences to anyone and neither should you! Enjoy and be comforted by your angel visitations and share them with people who appreciate them!

Pop stars and TV personalities freely talk about their own belief in guardian angels these days, and openly discuss their personal experiences. This makes it easier for the rest of us to share the miraculous experiences which have happened to us, the many millions of ordinary folk around the world. But of course, you don't have to be famous to have an angel story of your own. These anecdotes come from all countries and all cultures, and seem to occur to people of all religions, all ages and both sexes. Angels are for everyone and you have a guardian angel of your own.

How do we know they are around us?

'All God's angels come to us disguised.'
JAMES RUSSELL LOWELL

Angels show their presence in many different ways – most of them very subtle indeed – but this one was not so subtle to Victoria!

Many people believe that butterflies are a sign of spirit, and butterflies (especially unusual colours) seem to appear in times of stress and grief. Sometimes they even appear at times of year when they really shouldn't! And butterflies of no known variety are seen at times when we are looking for comfort. Are butterflies angels in disguise?

Little Victoria received her angelic message loud and clear!

BUTTERFLIES

'My daughter Denise walked away with a broken hand from a hundred-mile-an-hour-impact road accident in December last year.

For days before her accident, her 5-year-old daughter Victoria was obsessed with drawing butterflies and even asked her granddad to draw some.

A week before her accident Denise had seen a Red Admiral butterfly in her daughter's bedroom. She put it out of the window. On the day of her accident she collected her jeans from the washing line and was about to iron them when a Red Admiral flew out of them.

After the accident, her husband Tim picked up her belongings from the police compound – she opened her shopping bag and found Victoria's drawing of a butterfly inside it.

> *Denise had not realized the drawing was in her bag until that moment.*
>
> *Talking it over with her husband after the accident, Victoria, who was listening, said, "Mummy, there wasn't one butterfly, there were a hundred." Victoria put her hands together as if in prayer and said that one butterfly flew out and said, "We must pray for her and save her," and they all lifted her up.'*

This beautiful story just touched my heart. Could it possibly be true? Why would it not be?

One of the more common ways our guardian angels show themselves is by leaving gifts of 'angel feathers'. Do the feathers actually come from the wings of an angel? Who knows, but humankind has believed for many thousands of years that angels have wings and the angels know this! Those perfect little curled white feathers are the most common. Feathers are light and easy for angels to manifest for us – what a perfect sign – so maybe that is why they are among the commonest angel signs.

Barbara was finding life a little stressful. Was her feather a message from her angels? She did wonder!

CARPET FEATHER

'I walked along my hallway and saw a white speck on the carpet. Each time I passed over it I was aware of it. It really stood out. I thought I should vacuum it up but after I vacuumed, I realized it was still there! I felt annoyed and bent down to remove it and imagine my surprise when I found my white speck was really a feather! It was perfect. A small, fluffy and creamy white feather! I decided to keep it and put it in a little box on my dressing table. My answer had come.'

This next story is also subtle, but might this be the angels? This lady did ask for her sign after all.

FEATHERS ON THE BEACH

'First, let me tell you that I do believe in angels and once when things where not going well in my life I called out to them for a sign. I was walking along a local beach when I noticed that the sand was full of little white feathers. They were small and delicate, and at first I thought they were from a sea bird that had been washed up … but there were no other remains.'

Another lady watched a television programme about angels and although she was sceptical she decided to ask her angels to give her evidence of their existence by producing feathers as they had suggested on the programme. Not really thinking that anything would happen, she went for a walk and was amazed when she turned a corner to find pure white fluffy feathers every few yards along the whole stretch of the road.

Later on that day she went out for a second walk and this time she picked up one of the feathers and clutched it in her hand with the intention of taking it home – but when she opened her palm it had vanished.

One writer, Eileen, watched me on ITV's television programme *This Morning* and she was prompted to write to me about her own experience.

A FEATHER FROM THE OTHER SIDE?

Eileen and her husband had tragically lost their son in a car accident and, in their grief, had been to visit a highly respected psychic medium in the hope of making contact with him.

The medium said she felt that she had got in touch with him. She explained to the grieving parents that their son was going to leave them a feather as a sign and that as soon as he had done so they were to give her a telephone call to confirm it. Kenny, Eileen's husband, was a bit of a sceptic and hadn't really expected anything at all.

A short time later Kenny had been working in the garage and everything he touched seemed to go wrong. He decided to stop for a break and stood on the porch, but as he stood there daydreaming, a little white feather came floating down from nowhere. Kenny just put out his hand as it gently fell and then looked all around to see if he could see a bird that might have dropped it. He also checked the garden to see if other feathers were blowing around outside but he found nothing which would explain the feather appearing from nowhere.

The couple firmly believe that their son had made contact in the way that the medium suggested that he would, and that he chose his father to receive the 'message' personally because he was the one who needed the contact and the proof the most.

How quickly can they respond? Sometimes very fast indeed, as Sue discovered.

A FEATHER ON THE ROAD
APPEARS TO COMMAND!

'Someone messaged me on my mobile phone to say that if I believed in angels I should ask for a sign. They mentioned that white feathers are sometimes shown so I decided to give it a go.

On my way back from town today, with the message on my mind, I got stuck in a traffic jam and said, 'Ok, go ahead. I do believe in angels so show me, prove it to me, show me a white feather, a definite white feather – and do it soon!'

I started moving away in the traffic, and there, about 200 yards in front of me, stuck in the ground on the roadside was a HUGE white feather! Needless to say, I swore quite a lot with the shock of it.

I'm still not sure what to make of it. But if it was a coincidence, then it was an odd one!'

Bronwen was naturally distressed when her dog passed over but she was comforted by the sign she received.

AN ANGEL FEATHER SIGN
FROM MY DOG

'I lost my dog yesterday and was very distressed as he was a large part of my family's life and I shall be lost without him. But that evening I was watching a man who was walking in front of me when I spotted a white feather stuck to his clothes. And then this morning on my desk at work, and goodness knows where it came from, was a purple feather!

I really believe that this is a sign that he is still with me or that an Angel is aware of my sadness and is trying to help.'

Jayne believes that this baby was being looked over by her own guardian angel as another feather appeared.

AN ANGEL WATCHING OVER A NEW BORN BABY GIRL

'One of the mums at the school where I work gave birth to a little girl who almost immediately had to travel to another hospital, without mum, for a heart operation.

A few weeks later mum brought her elder daughter to collect her baby sister from hospital. There was a complication though. The doctors were very concerned because there appeared to be a bowel problem and the family were told their precious daughter would have to face another operation.

We were all worried but I was lucky enough to get the opportunity to hold the little girl. I believe in angels and

---

> *whilst I was holding the baby I noticed how small and frail she was. But I knew she was being looked after when a single downy white feather floated down a few feet away and landed on the ground. I realized the angels were with us. I'm pleased to announce that the little girl has since started gaining weight and is very healthy … oh, and the bowel complication was a false alarm!'*

Feathers are well known as angel calling cards. Everywhere I go people love to tell me about their angel feather stories. One surprised lady found a feather in her saucer under her coffee cup and another lady found an angel feather in the freezer at work. One feather turned up in a previously unopened plastic shopping bag at the supermarket. It seems the more unlikely locations feel more like real angel encounters. You would be surprised at how many people carry their feathers around with them. I've been shown feathers in purses and wallets, in little pouches and stuck to pieces of cardboard and carried around in handbags!

Are all feathers angel feathers?

Angel feathers are a powerful reminder of angelic presence and people hold their own 'messages' close to their hearts. One lady has an angel feather jar and collects these little treasures every-where she goes. Another contact told me about her feather box which she keeps by the bed and feathers are often stored in people's jewellery boxes and hat boxes! I often wonder why some people have quite so many feathers. Do you think that by keeping these angelic mementos it encourages more signs to come their way? I feel sure it does.

Recently, I have been teaching a regular angel class in my local town. The group had been together for many weeks and with Christmas fast approaching I promised them that we would do an angel related Christmas craft on the final night.

I had the idea to create some laminated bookmarks and collected a few bits and pieces together. I placed the felt pens, sparkly paper and angel confetti together in envelopes and placed everything in a single box. It was then that I decided to collect a few feathers together so that people could laminate them directly into their bookmarks.

It was too late for me to contact people to bring their own angel feathers so I decided to drive to a local village where swans frequented the banks of a little stream. Just as I had hoped, the banks were covered in white feathers but sadly they were all wet and muddy from the recent rain. I was determined to collect some though and reached far down the sides of the bank to collect the best ones that I could – nearly falling in a couple of times in the process, I might add.

As I was collecting them I had the strange thought that all my hard work would be wasted and the feathers would be forgotten or something. I decided to put the thought far from my mind and carry on regardless, so I collected plenty of these soggy feathers.

When I got home I was upset at what I had collected as there was no way these feathers were beautiful enough for the task I had in mind. There was nothing for it but to wash them all! I tipped them all out into the bathroom sink and filled the bowl up with water. What seemed like half a bag of soil immediately fell to the bottom of the sink and I had to refill the sink – and again, two or three more times. Time was moving on and I had to dry these feathers, and quickly.

Grabbing a pair of old tights I carefully piled them into the toe and set about drying them with my hairdryer. Several of them flew out of the tights as I had not pushed them down far enough, and the feathers started flying around the bedroom. Were there going to be enough? It was funny, but I was too busy to laugh.

As I sat on the edge of my bed in despair I noticed a feather stuck on the side of my pillow – perhaps I could pull a few feathers through the side of my pillows and add them to the damp pile of feathers I had besides me? The feathers were a funny selection of shapes and none of them were very pretty. What on earth was I doing? But this was part of my craft, and so I plucked a few more through the side of the pillow and shoved the whole lot into a plastic sandwich bag and put them carefully into the box along with the other craft items.

With only moments to go, I got into the car and drove to my destination. As I carried my box from the car to the door, I silently laughed to myself as a large white, perfectly curled feather sat on the doorstep of the shop, so I picked it up to present to the organizer and owner of the shop as a gift on my way in.

The group were already waiting for me as I rushed through the door and the organizer had kindly brought along some wine and mince pies … very festive. We were set for a fun night. When it was time to begin the craft, I began telling my story of the feathers, and how I had nearly fallen in the stream. Everyone giggled as I told them how I'd had the premonition that I would somehow forget the feathers, but that I was safe in the knowledge that they were tucked at the bottom of my box.

You can image my surprise then, when I lifted out all the craft items and put them onto the table. The feathers were nowhere to be seen! Embarrassed, I went back out to the car to see if I had dropped them on the way or if perhaps they had fallen out, but I didn't find them.

I must have forgotten the feathers! But no one seemed to mind and carried on with the craft regardless. I contemplated the situation as I watched everyone enjoying their craft and then I realized why the feathers had disappeared. The answer came to me in a blinding flash! These feathers weren't angel feathers at all, but swan feathers! Real angel feathers appear when we most need them and I'd gone out of my way to create a false situation. My intent was pure but just the same, these were not real angel feathers.

You know I never did find the feathers that I'd worked so hard to collect and I searched everywhere at home when I got back. Are angel feathers just ordinary feathers that we happen to find when we are out and about? Apparently not! Angel feathers are gifts from our loving protectors. 'Any old feather' (even if they are very beautiful) just won't do!

I couldn't resist sharing this one last angel feather story with you.

IRENE'S ANGEL

Irene had always believed that she had her own guardian angel but she never really thought much about them until she began reading about them in magazines. Irene started to search the internet to see if she could find any stories about them, and after a few months she began to understand more and wanted to believe she really did have an angel watching over her.

Irene is a nurse at Wycombe Hospital, and one morning when she was getting her car out of the garage to go to work, she says that she could not believe her eyes when she opened the car door. On the actual hinge of the door there sat a lovely white feather! Irene felt that the feather must have been placed there as there was no way that it could have got there on its own, and it would have blown off when she opened the door.

About three weeks later Irene's car was broken into at work. The window was smashed and part of the radio was taken. But Irene believes that her angel had been protecting her by ensuring that she was not in the car at the time. She says that it might seem a strange thing to believe but she feels sure that this is the truth.

Irene also told me that her parents and her little sister are on 'the other side'. She visits the graves on a regular basis and feels that they are around her a lot. Irene visited the graves recently to commemorate what would have been her Dad's birthday. Her family are all buried in the same cemetery and on this particular day, after placing the flowers on her father's grave she found a white feather. There were no other feathers around and Irene firmly believes the feather was a sign for her that they were safe in the afterlife.

I'm sure that she is right because many people find white feathers on graves after asking for a sign, and they are comforted to know that the angels are looking after their loved ones.

Have you ever felt the urge to lie down on the grass and look up at the moving clouds in the sky above you? Clouds can be magical and so many of us are able to see pictures in the moving shapes …

Angel clouds

Nicole was sitting in class one day when she caught sight of a cloud which began to change shape rather rapidly. Nothing unusual in that – the wind will often blow clouds into unusual shapes – but Nicole was watching the cloud form into the shape of a woman, who then 'grew wings!' And Nicole is not the only one!

Visiting her daughter in England about five years ago, Samantha and her loved ones went out and cut their Christmas tree ready for the big day.

It had snowed the night before and she said it was the most beautiful sparkling snow. Her granddaughters had never made snow angels before so they all lay down in the perfect snow together and moved their arms and legs backwards and forwards making the shape of the wings.

As they lay down in the snow, clouds drifted past in the beautiful blue sky. Nicole thought that she saw angels formed in the clouds above them. Wondering if she was the only one she asked the grandchildren if they could see any patterns in the clouds. And you can guess what they saw. They all agreed that they could see four perfectly formed angel clouds; a reflection of the four of them lying down in the snow perhaps? And a memory the family would never forget.

I remember reading about some angel cloud experiences on the internet and decided to ask my own angels to give me an 'angel cloud' before the end of the day. I decided to take my camera out with me when we went on a long drive later in the day. As the sun started to go down, beautiful colours flooded the sky and I had high expectations of taking the perfect angel photo. Beautiful streamers of white flooded through the pinks, lilacs and golds as the sun began to set, but nothing felt like an angel cloud to me, beautiful though it was.

Slightly disappointed that I had not found my angel cloud by the time I went home I mulled over my high expectations of the day. Had I asked for too much? Was it not possible to create these things on demand?

I got into bed and picked up the new magazine on my bedside table to console myself with a good read before drifting off to sleep, but even I was surprised when I realized the subject of the first article I read – it was someone's experience of seeing an angel cloud! The clock was just five to midnight. I had my angel cloud after all … just through the eyes of another!

> 'A man on the street is pointing up to the sky.
> "Look, an Angel!" he yells.
> Passers-by laugh. "You fool, that is only a cloud."
> How wonderful it would be to see angels where there
> are only clouds. How sad it would be to see only
> clouds where there are angels.'

ANONYMOUS

Orbs

'Orbs' – those balls of light we pick up on our digital cameras – are sometimes believed to be signs of guardian angels. Associated more with ghosts or spirits, we don't currently have a full scientific explanation for these circular lights. 'Orbs' are not just picked up on digital cameras. People film them moving on video tape and they are sometimes seen on photographs taken with older cameras using normal film.

What is the difference between a ghost and an angel? Ghosts are believed to be the energy forms of human beings who are moving around our earth plane. Some ghosts are human souls with consciousness and others are energy memory of souls that once lived on earth. Angels, on the other hand, are pure loving consciousness and have never been human but are directly sent from God to protect and watch over humankind … among other things!

Orbs are often photographed at supposed haunted locations but there does seem to be a difference as to when and where these images are captured. People have sent me photographs of school children under their care who are going through difficult times in their lives. These orb shapes of a variety of colours can be seen almost hovering over the top of the child. Might these be relatives in spirit or guardian angels watching over the child in need?

> *'See that you do not look down on one of these little ones. For I tell you that their angels in heaven always see the face of my father in heaven.'*
> MATTHEW 18:10

Another photograph that someone kindly shared with me showed the outline of a woman in a bright orb of light. The photograph was taken during a Christmas dinner when the family had asked their grandma in spirit to join them at the dinner table. It certainly seemed like the shape of a woman to me.

I have a great photo at home with a large orb on it. It was taken just a week ago. My daughter was messing around and taking loads of photos of me in our living room. After taking about 50 photos on our digital camera I suddenly had an idea. I asked her to pose with her great uncle Eric (a bit of a joke as my uncle is on the 'other side' but a very active spiritual presence in our family!).

My daughter Charlotte posed for the camera and held out her arms as if she was hugging someone. We laughed a lot when we downloaded the images to our computer. Immediately behind her was the largest orb of light I had ever seen. Was this 'Uncle Eric', our family guardian angel, jumping into the photo? What is extra funny is that the orb is behind my daughter, not actually in the place where she held her arms out. It just goes to show that you can't control everything! Strangely, nothing appeared on any of the other 50 or so photographs that she had taken immediately before my request. Was this a coincidence? You decide!

Sparkles

One of the letters I received on my website was from a lady who saw 'angel sparkles' in her room on the evening before her brother passed over. Was this a sign from heaven that he was being collected and taken 'home'? People see these sparkling lights for all sorts of reasons, so don't worry if you have seen them too! They appear during impending birth, during family parties and get-togethers and during special occasions in our lives. As with the other experiences like feathers and lights, these sparkles are usually accompanied by a feeling of great love and warmth.

Emma wrote, 'It's my belief that angels will appear to us in the way that we can most easily perceive them, and possibly at different stages of our development their visual appearance may actually change.'

I am inclined to agree with this statement. Emma went on to explain, '… during the initial stages of my development I started to see a bright blue light flashing at me which would often obscure and interrupt my normal vision. I asked many people what this might mean, but none of their answers felt quite right for me. I also came to feel very quickly that Archangel Michael worked with and watched over healers, although traditionally I know that Raphael is associated with healing.'

Emma is right but I always say that if you feel a different angel is working with you on specific tasks then you must go with your own intuition because you are probably right! I know several healers that work with Archangel Michael and Archangel Gabriel.

She says, 'It wasn't until last year that I learnt that this blue light is often associated with Michael, and when I read this I got the familiar tug of intuition and deep-seated knowing that this was connected. This also coincided with a period of cleansing for me and Gabriel's name kept coming into my mind, and I also started seeing a white flashing light. Someone read to me from a book, that white light was associated with Gabriel, and Gabriel was associated with cleansing and purity, which resulted in another feeling of connection.

'Not long after that I was doing a reading for someone who works with angels herself and as I turned to the room at the side of where we were sitting, there was a seven-to-eight-feet-tall figure, which I knew instinctively was an angel, although there wasn't a great deal of clarity to what I was seeing, but a vague white and gold light. Over the next few months I had several more external visions whereby an image of the "stereotypical" angel with wings flashed up at me, with more clarity, as pure white light surrounded by gold. I still see Michael's blue light flashing too.'

And again, different people see different colours (not necessarily those which are traditionally associated with particular angels.) So, go with your own instincts.

Emma believes that as we develop and our vibrations increase, the clarity grows, and also the culture within which we are raised might also determine how we perceive their vibration and the form in which they manifest, so that they are recognizable to us.

> '*Angels are intelligent reflections of light, that original light which has no beginning. They can illuminate. They do not need tongues or ears, for they can communicate without speech, in thought.*'
>
> JOHN OF DAMASUS

White Shadows

Do you ever catch a swirly mist out of the corner of your eye? This might be spirit or angels – or it could be just plain old smoke! Never discount the obvious with any of these experiences because not everything is paranormal!

However, white cloudy shapes are often captured on camera too. I saw a fabulous flash of white light on a wedding photograph. It was 'sitting' between the bride and her mother – in the position that the bride's father would have sat if he had not died a few months earlier. It makes you think doesn't it? Was this light a wedding guest from the other side?

One visitor to my website sent me a photograph of one of these great shadow pictures. The family had just finished hanging 'angel bear' decorations on the wall at home, and taken a photograph of the new Christmas decorations. The image showed a white mist in front, which was shaped like an angel.

He immediately asked other family members what they thought of the white shadowy shape and they all agreed that it looked just like an angel. I was so convinced, I added the image to my website!

Another photograph came through to my email tonight, but this photograph is a little more private so I have decided to keep her name a secret. One distressed lady was taking a photograph of her beautiful daughter who was struggling with a weight disorder and also severe food allergies. The poor girl had lost a lot of weight and the mother wanted to show her daughter how badly she needed to gain a few pounds by photographing her in just a T-shirt and her underwear. Yet her daughter is almost completely obscured by a white streak which goes from the top of her head right down to her feet and she told me that she just knows the angels exist. This lady has a special angel altar at home which she regularly uses as a place of worship, and this is a big help to her. The angels certainly made their presence known here.

You can easily create a special corner at home where you can make a little angel altar with a small picture of an angel or a little figurine and then fill your space with some special objects like crystals, flowers and photographs of loved ones. For more information about angel altars, read my book, *An Angel Treasury* (also published by HarperElement).

> *'The proof if heaven be, or only seem,*
> *That we forever choose what we will dream!'*
> HELEN HUNT JACKSON

Rainbows

How many people 'see' rainbows as a sign from the afterlife and beyond? Many associate the passage from this life to the next with rainbows, especially with animals. Rainbows are associated with bridges from one plane of existence to another.

The film *The Wizard of Oz* has become a classic and the song 'Somewhere over the Rainbow' is arguably the most popular song to come from the film. The words tell us that somewhere over the rainbow there is '… a land that I heard of, once in a lullaby'. It seems to express the fact that people have some distant memory of this rainbow land but can't quite remember it! Many people feel that they are visiting the earth from our real 'home' over the rainbow. The rainbow has become a symbol for 'the other side' and people see their loved ones as well as angels coming from this place. Here is a rainbow inspired experience:

MONA'S RAINBOWS

'In August 2002 my dear friend Mona passed away. I feel she has sent me many signs.

A few weeks later I hired some videos. I hadn't really thought about my choices but was surprised at the coincidences I had found. One was the film Pearl Harbor, and Mona and her recent boyfriend had taken a trip to Hawaii when she found out her cancer was back. Both of them had really wanted to see Pearl Harbor.

The other movie I picked up was The Judy Garland Story. Well, I never even thought about this until she started singing the song "Somewhere over the Rainbow".

I cried buckets after this; you see Mona refused to make plans for her funeral but she did say she wanted this song. I hadn't known it was a special song for Mona and I have *always loved it myself. It was one of my favourite songs, and one I sang when I was little and pretending to be a singer.*

Then in September I went to visit my friend Carol. It had begun to rain but when I got there, Carol called from the kitchen for me to come and see the beautiful rainbow. Because of the rain we were unable to have our planned bonfire, so our other friend Rosemary (a jazz singer) started singing in the living room. Since I had to get back to town to meet my friends, she asked me if there were any songs I would like her to sing. She didn't know the ones I picked or have the music, but she said she had a song in her head all day as she was driving over. She began singing "Somewhere over the Rainbow!"

Later, when I left, I noticed it wasn't wet anywhere else. It was like it had only rained over her house!

About a month after this I visited friends in hospital; they are also singers. I was telling them about this and they said they had seen the rainbow too. They live by a lake and were out walking on the nearby train track – the rainbow they saw was big and bright and lasted such a long time.

So I feel now whenever I see a rainbow that it's a message from Mona and she's okay.'

How do other people see angels?

I was interested to see how other people see angels in their lives. You can see how many different ways people experience them and this is by no means a comprehensive list! Mysterious birds and animals appearing out of nowhere, not being afraid when they surely should, or just hanging around a lot feature in some other stories!

Let's look at some experiences.

RACHEL'S ANGELS

A lovely lady called Rachel told me that she sees her angels towering over clients when she does readings for them. Rachel says that some of the angels are as tall as eight or nine feet.

She says that sometimes they glow with faint golden, silver or white light, and at other times, they appear to her as normal people. But there is always this ethereal air about them; just by their appearance you can see they have never been of this world, their eyes are slightly too big and beautiful and their build is of a proportion that just can't be of the physical. Their whole appearance is a slightly exaggerated form of how we look.

She says that the angels she has seen as she goes about her own daily business are different – the ones who walk among us in life she sees most often as pale cream or beige coloured from top to toe – hair, skin, clothing – and they are always slender, without wings as often as she sees them with wings.

Rachel sees angels at the side of the road as she drives to work. She says that the route is quite rural and scary, but she's not afraid because she sees the angels out of the corner of her eye as eight-foot pale winged people by the roadside!

She told me that she never used to believe in angels, even calling herself 'the sceptic', until she saw one almost two years ago with her own eyes during a psychic reading for a lady who had lost her son. The angel was standing behind the client with his hands on her shoulders, and he was fiercely beautiful, almost scary looking.

Rachel says that for her, that first sighting opened a floodgate, because after that she was able to see them quite often.

Amazing! Another lady wrote that she has twice fallen over but found herself being caught in midair! She feels that there is no way that she could have held herself in midair in that way unless she was being caught by angels. She even believes that she was held for such a long time in this position that she could easily have been photographed in this way!

Many said that they asked their angels to watch over their loved ones at night. One lady said that she felt the angels fly out to her family and friends with love and protection. People felt angels with them when they asked for them to be around and found they reacted to this contact with tears of joy or pleasure.

One person wrote of a premonition that they were going to have a motorcycle accident. On the morning of the accident they were nervous and could feel a presence reminding them to be careful. The presence also suggested they ride a different way to the others in the group but this person decided to ignore the feeling and instead follow the other motorcyclists.

Scarily, this person did have the predicted collision and hit an oncoming car on a bad bend, but said that they felt as if someone was holding and protecting them. The car was a write-off but the motorcycle rider survived with a damaged foot and a broken laptop. Someone was certainly being protected on that day.

Frances wrote and told me about the birth of her last grandchild.

ANGELS AT THE BIRTH

Frances told me she was in the delivery room and that it was approximately 12.15pm, when she saw her family's angels. Her son, she recalls, was on one side of the bed, holding his wife's Claire's hand, and she was on the other side doing the same. She says that she looked up at her son and smiled, and then noticed that standing beside him was his Guardian Angel.

Frances says that she definitely knew it was his Guardian Angel. Her son is six feet tall and his guardian angel appeared to be about eight feet tall. The angel was a whitish colour but appeared in a sort of silhouette. Then she saw another angel hovering over her daughter-in-law lying on the bed. Claire's guardian angel was the same colour and also appeared as a silhouette.

A few minutes later Frances's grandchild Kiron was born. Claire started to cry, and as her son was comforting his wife, Frances went to look at the new baby, who was being looked after by a midwife. Frances was thrilled to see that hovering over the new baby's cot was yet another guardian angel.

Frances did not immediately share with her family what she had seen and said that she waited until the following evening before she felt able to share her experience. Frances said that she wasn't frightened by this special privilege and, in fact, it seemed the most natural thing in the world.

Frances was lucky enough to see an angel on another occasion too. She was sitting quietly on a bench at the end of her garden. It was a beautiful moment and she says that every blade of grass, and each flower petal, was bright and sparkling and so vivid whilst she was sitting there.

It was at that time that she was aware of a presence standing beside her. She says that out of the corner of her eye, she saw the Virgin Mary, yet she also knew she was an Angel.

Frances turned her head and could only see the brightest, whitest light she had ever seen, yet it didn't hurt her eyes. She didn't blink or shade her eyes. As she sat there, she was enjoying the peace and love until she realized that this special angel had gone. At a friend's house later she shared her special experience. Frances's friend told her that the Virgin Mary is the Queen of the Angels.

Landreth has seen angels several times. He has seen them in dreams and also once whilst wide awake. One day when he and his wife were watching television, he saw a massive angel (although his wife saw nothing at the time). The angel was very large and outlined in golden light. He says it was there and gone in just a moment.

He recalls that the angel was massive and only part of the angel was visible. He said he had the impression that this angel could easily have been bigger than the room itself.

So what do they look like? Are we any nearer to the truth? Mohammed had a vision of the Archangel Michael when he was alone in the sea. He saw the angel 'perfect in Majesty, Glory and Beauty'. Later he saw angels which were made of ice and even fire!

Emanuel Swedenborg, the well-known scientist (1688–1772), regularly saw angels in dreams and visions and described them as being love, light and wisdom. He stated that they breathe (a special air) and that they also speak and write. He believed, though, that the reason we could see angels at all was because they 'took on' a material body for our benefit. There is more on Swedenborg's amazing visions in Chapter 6.

> *'I saw them with my bodily eyes as clearly as I see you.*
> *And when they departed, I used to weep and wish they*
> *would take me with them.'*
>
> SAINT JOAN OF ARC

Rather frightening, though, is the description by the prophet Ezekiel who had a vision in which he saw four angels. These angels appeared like men, but with each one having four faces and four wings. They had feet like calves' hooves and human hands under their wings, and they also sparkled like the colour of brass! This is not really how we see angels in the modern day and, despite the many hundreds of emails and letters I receive every month, I have never once had someone see an angel in this way. But that could be to ease our own fear, of course.

The Reverend Billy Graham states that, 'angels have a beauty and variety that surpass anything known to men.' And I'm sure he's right. So what do I think of angels?

JACKY'S VIEW OF ANGELS

Personally? I see angels as beings of pure light and love on a vibration which resonates higher than our own. This vibration makes it impossible for us to see them normally, but unlike us I believe that on occasion, angels can and do slow down this vibration so that we can see them either in their natural form or in a form which is comforting to us.

Sometimes we see angels as human beings and at other times as beings beyond our understanding. No matter how they appear people always seems to know that they have encountered an angel, which means that they are not just 'seen' but in someway 'felt' by the human soul.

Angels don't always appear in the way we expect. Keep your eyes, ears and everything else open for an encounter with an angel.

'The golden moments in the stream of life rush past us
and we see nothing but sand; the angels come to visit us,
and we only know them when they are gone.'

GEORGE ELIOT

a little angel healing

'The wisdom of the ages teaches that each individual …
has a personal Guardian Angel with him or her at
every moment of life's journey.'
JANICE T. CONNELL, *ANGEL POWER*

Communication is the key with all things. Keep asking your angels for their help with your personal wellbeing and healing.

'The very presence of an angel is a communication.
Even when an angel crosses our path in silence, God has
said to us, "I am here. I am present in your life."'
TOBIAS PALMER

Can angels help with healing? Well, they can and do, it seems! They help with little things and much bigger ones too. Is an earache too small a task to ask the angels for help with? Not at all! I remember sitting on a train once with the most awful earache. It was late at night and I was the only one in the carriage. I was nearing my last stop and I'm not sure if there was even anyone else on the train, but I certainly didn't have a painkiller in my bag and I was desperate. There was nothing else I could do except ask for my angel's help and, amazingly, after just a few minutes the pain had completely disappeared.

Archangel Raphael is traditionally associated with healing, so this lady asked for help directly from the healing angel, but she could also have just called on the best angel for the job.

ANGELS HELP WITH EARACHE

'I've had a cold coming on in the last week or so and last night while visiting my grandma, my ear suddenly became uncomfortably blocked up. It was actually very painful and my ear felt like it wanted to pop but wouldn't.

So last night I prayed to Raphael and asked him to heal my ear. I woke up this morning and it was all gone. I feel a lot better.'

Tanya is now 21 and engaged to be married, but when she was ill as a child her mother decided to take the angels on. Don't forget, angels don't only come when we are dying but for many hundreds of reasons. In this instance, I believe they were helping the young child, not collecting her!

NOT HER TIME

'When I was about three years old we were living with some family friends while our house was being built. My mother tells me that I had a massive fever, and that the doctors seemed unable do anything to reduce it. My mother was a senior staff nurse at the same hospital at the time and I guess seeing other youngsters ill and dying she was especially sensitive about her own daughter.

I was in the bedroom with mum and dad, and crying my little three-year-old eyes out when I suddenly stopped crying. With a huge smile on my face I began looking at the ceiling above the door.

"Mummy, look at the angels! The angels are here!" I called out.

My mother was not amused! She isn't really one to

believe in the paranormal but dad said to me later that she started screaming at the door saying, "Leave my baby alone … it's not her time."

They must have agreed because I'm still here alive and well!'

One lady remembers a time when she saw a white ray of light shaped like wings, which often shimmered around her husband or shot towards his knee when he suffered from his recurring pain in that area.

Angels associated with healing

Do you need help with healing? All angels can help, but for specific expertise, ask for the following:

Emotional healing – Archangels Ariel, Raguel and Gabriel Media

Assistance during pregnancy and childbirth – Archangels Gabriel, Raphael and Sandalphon

Broken Bones – Archangel Michael

Grief and dying – Archangels Azrael and Raphael

General health and healing – Archangels Metatron and Raphael

'From beyond the blue, an angel came and held
his lighted body over the wounded soldier. Behold!
You are healed dear one.'

ANONYMOUS

As with all angelic assistance, asking your angels for their help is the key to receiving their involvement. Ask the angels and then know that their help will come. You might like to call on one of the angels above directly. If you need emotional support when going for a consultation with your doctor or surgeon, then call on the Archangel Gabriel.

Caroline reads my column and wrote to share her own healing story.

FAMILY HEALING ANGELS

'One night about three weeks ago I woke up at 3am with a horrendous stomach pain (I suffer with IBS and the pain woke me). I was in agony so I asked for the healing angels to take the pain away. Moments later I saw seven figures in the corner of our bedroom near the window. They were all in a line behind one another!

The first angel was a purple violet colour but the others were white and they were very tall, around seven feet. The vision only lasted for a few minutes but soon afterwards I fell sound asleep and woke up pain free. It was a fantastic experience.'

Remember the golden rule when working with angels – ask, ask, ask for their help and tell them what you need!

> *'Make yourself familiar with the angels, and behold them*
> *frequently in spirit; for without being seen, they are*
> *present with you.'*
> SAINT FRANCIS DE SALES

3

protection and safe keeping

'For it is written. He shall give His angels

charge of thee, to keep thee.'

LUKE 4:10

Although for many people the idea of a guardian angel seems little more than a fairy tale, lots of people can imagine that angels are real beings. A poll in *TIME* magazine showed that 69 per cent of people believe in angels.

Angels are well known for their role as protectors and guardians of humankind. It's nice not to feel alone, isn't it? I've read the most amazing stories of people being lifted up in the air and gently placed in positions of safety, and other stories where a strong urge to do, or not to do something resulted in a lifesaving action. Does this message come from our own guardian angels?

'Angel of God, My Guardian dear,
To whom God's love entrusts me here;
Ever this day be at my side,
To light and guard,
To rule and guide.'

TRADITIONAL ANGEL PRAYER

Angels do not follow our laws of time and space, so acts which seem miraculous to us may be more normal to them. They do seem able to save lives on certain occasions (although why not on every occasion still remains a mystery). 'There are far more things on heaven and earth …' as the saying goes. Maybe we are not meant to understand 'everything'. We have to assume a greater plan.

It's as if the angels have some prior knowledge of what's coming up for us and are able to assist in keeping us from harm. With no rules over physical time, are they aware of dangers which are coming up?

Anna responded to my newsletter request for personal stories of angel intervention. Angels often assist in car accidents like this one.

SAVED BY ANGELS – TWICE!

'I've had a couple of experiences for which I can find no other explanation other than the fact that I was protected in some way. I like to think they were angels. Both occurred while I was driving, which (to my knowledge anyway) are the only times I have been in real danger.

The first occasion was fourteen years ago when a vehicle

which was coming in the opposite direction appeared over the brow of a hill on the wrong side of the road. It hit my car, which then overturned twice before landing upside down in a ditch. I had two passengers and my dog in the car as well. As the car overturned, I felt as if I was 'wrapped up' in something warm and completely protected from what was happening.

All of us, including my dog, walked out of that accident without injury. The other driver careered off the road into a tree stump … but also walked away uninjured. Both cars were complete write-offs. I often look at the photos of the car and marvel that we all walked away.

The second occasion was even more miraculous. I was driving along the city bypass in the outside lane and could see that the traffic was coming to a halt in both lanes ahead of me. The inside lane was stationary as I stopped in the outside lane. I looked into my rear view mirror and saw a car coming up very fast behind me. He seemed to be driving very erratically.

At this point, "someone else" took control of the car, and I can only believe it was my guardian angel. There was nowhere for me to escape to. The inside lane was solid with traffic. There were no gaps for me to slot into and to my side was an oil tanker.

In a split second, the steering wheel was turned sharply to the left for me and a gap appeared on the inside lane between the tanker and the car in front of it. Before I knew what had happened, I was safely in this gap. It all happened so quickly, and there was no way I could have thought about what to do and completed the manoeuvre in such a short time. It was definitely done for me.

I know my angels helped me to avoid a serious accident that day.'

Jewelle Saint James, the author of *All You Need is Love*, also had a driving angel.

JEWELLE'S DRIVING ANGEL

'*I was happily driving along a four-lane road on the way to our local town and I remember there was absolutely no traffic in any direction.*

All of a sudden, out of nowhere a voice told me to move over one lane. I had no idea where the voice was coming from but it was loud and insistent. "Why?" I argued with the voice, "There's no traffic."

"Just move and do it NOW," the voice insisted.

"Okay, okay," I sighed, feeling foolish changing lanes on an empty street. But seconds later a car (being pushed by two men in an attempt to jump-start their vehicle),

appeared out of nowhere, just as I passed by. Since I had already changed to an inner lane I only had to breezily drive by.

If the voice had not told me to move I would have ploughed right into the other car.'

It's funny, but this 'arguing with the unseen voice' is a classic way of knowing that this inner voice is actually separate from ourselves. I did this myself as a child when I found myself being swept out to sea. I heard this inner voice tell me that I could drown if I wanted to (a preposterous idea) or 'they could help me back to shore'. I remember arguing with the voice that I could not swim but as you can gather, I was assisted back to shore and made it safely without drowning. The choice was always mine but it seemed bizarre to have a conversation with something I could not see.

I also remember hearing an insistent voice telling me to pull over to the side of the road several times, and arguing with the voice that I would scratch my new vehicle on the hedge which ran alongside. Luckily, I agreed because the act saved me from being smashed into by a van driving at speed in the middle of the road. Both these stories are told in full in my book *An Angel Treasury*. If you hear a voice which warns you of urgent danger, then it's worth paying attention!

At a recent workshop I began by asking people about their own personal experiences relating to angels and all things mystical. I normally discover around three quarters of the people present have a 'weird, unexplainable moment' in their lives and often they believe them to be associated with angel intervention.

On a motorbike trip, one lady and her husband were involved in a serious accident and they were thrown from their bike. By rights, she explained they should have been killed as they were on a very busy road, but both of them were unharmed. Even so, they were taken to hospital for a check up.

In the ambulance her husband was very shocked indeed, but not because of the accident which had just occurred. It seems that both of them were lifted off the busy road and laid gently down on the kerb in a place of safety away from the traffic immediately after the accident happened. Yet neither of them had any awareness of how this might have happened. The ambulance crew also had no idea as no one else was at the scene at the time! But my workshop attendee had her own interpretation of how it might have happened – angelic intervention! Sometimes these things really are a mystery, aren't they?

Here is another one:

FLYING

'Call me silly, but I have always had a fascination with angels. As a child I always felt their presence, and one of my favourite pictures was of an angel watching over a child crossing a bridge. I've had some close calls in my life and I know it was the touch of an angel that made me stop at the moment which meant life or death.

I was once in an automobile accident where six cars were damaged beyond repair. During the accident I was knocked unconscious and when I woke up I was hanging onto a car door, flying through the air and heading towards another parked car. I remember screaming, "I don't want to die," and it was as if a flash of bright light came between me and that car, and I felt my body being put in an upright position.

I never hit the ground or even the car and in fact I just

> *ended up standing in the middle of the street! The police were surprised that I was alive with just a bump on my head from where I had hit the windshield on the way through. It seems totally bizarre now when I look back on it – I can't imagine how I could have landed so safely.*
>
> *I know in my heart that my angel came to my rescue that day and that angels have always been by my side.'*

At one of my angel workshops, a woman shared a strange experience of her own, but this one happened whilst she was giving birth.

She and her baby were in grave danger and she remembers being clipped and hooked up to all sorts of machinery during the delivery. Yet all the while this panic was going on around her she was feeling calm and reassured.

She didn't immediately register that she was in an 'out of body' position, floating on the ceiling above the action. She said she was actually watching 'the woman' give birth on the bed below her! The baby was born just in time and had the cord wrapped dangerously around its neck. The doctors and nurses worked quickly and the baby was fine in no time at all.

After all the pressure was over the lady dropped back into her body again, almost as if she no longer needed to be taken 'away' from the trauma of the birth for a few minutes! She feels that her angels were keeping her away from the pain of the birth.

Sue went through a very difficult time in her life and she was sure that the vision she experienced was an angel coming to reassure her that everything would be okay.

ANGELS COMFORTED ME

'I lost a baby at nine weeks and subsequently fell pregnant soon afterwards with twins. I had reached almost four months before my husband and I started to celebrate but a week later I lost them and I was totally devastated. I just walked around for days in a state of shock. It was hard for us both and I struggled to come to terms with what had happened.

A week later, I was lying on my bed just staring at the ceiling. I was crying and kept asking "Why, why did this have to happen?"

It was then that I had a "vision". I saw a bright light and then the shadow of a lady in a long dress, and she appeared to be holding something. As she stepped forward I saw that she was carrying two babies. One baby I "knew" to be a girl.

She was the smallest with dark hair and the other was a boy - big and bouncy with blond hair.

She smiled and handed me the little boy. The second he was in my arms I had a flash in my mind of this chubby blond baby aged around six to nine months bursting through a wooden set of patio doors in a baby walker (in a room that I didn't recognize). He was squealing with laughter and had his hands in the air. I shook my head, and assumed delirium.

A few months later I fell pregnant again. It was a fraught pregnancy, full of anxiety, but right from the start I knew I was carrying a boy. I got through the pregnancy and everything was fine this time. I gave birth to a beautiful baby boy. He put on 1lb in the first few days and was very happy and healthy.

Then one day, when he was four months old, my husband built an extension. I hadn't told him about my vision but when my son was eight months old I was sat on the sofa and suddenly the wooden patio doors flew open and my son came flying through in his new baby walker, followed closely by his dad chasing him. It was the strangest feeling.

After all this time, my vision had come true. Not even I could deny that. I couldn't help feeling that my son had waited for me in order to be born, and that his sister needed to become stronger. Whether she comes back to me, or is born to someone else, I can't know yet. I've no plans to have another child at the moment, but I suppose I'll just have to wait and see.'

Angels often come to comfort us when we are grieving. It's as if they come to bring us hope of a brighter future. Many people tell me about the mysterious invisible 'being' who puts a reassuring hand upon their shoulder or seems to wrap them in a warm, supportive hug.

Strangely, angels are frequently felt when people are in the bath, whilst washing up or even during the ironing! They communicate easily at any of those times when we are alone doing tasks which allow our minds to wander. During these relaxed states, they seem to be able to reach us. The 'day-dreaming' mind is perfect for angel contact.

Of course, this also includes waiting at the checkout! Here's another story:

ANGELS CARRY GRANDDAD TO HEAVEN

'My grandfather lived in America and was gradually slipping from this life. My mum called me on the phone and I just cried all afternoon.

I so badly wanted to be with my mother and my grand-father but there was nothing I could do. Instead I went food shopping. I had to do something normal to take my mind off the devastating news.

While I was standing in the check-out line, I was feeling very sorry for myself, but when I looked up I saw this lovely, dark-skinned man smiling at me. I'm quite a shy person so immediately looked down but when I plucked up the courage to peek back up again it was as if he hadn't moved from the spot. He was still there smiling at me.

At the same time I could hear a voice telling me that everything was going to be all right, and for me not to cry because the angels were with my granddad and they would be with him to see him safely "home". They communicated with me that I was not to worry about my mum and that the angels would make sure that she was well looked after.

The man still smiled at me and he had a lovely purple glow about him and this time I smiled back at him. My son spoke to me so I turned away for a moment. As I finished talking to my son I looked up to see the man walking towards the door and then he just disappeared into thin air!

Even today, I believe that he was an angel sent to help me through the hurt of not being able to be at my grandfather's bedside as he was passing over.'

Andrea also feels angels around her family a lot, and she says that she is convinced that the Angels protect them all.

CAMPING ANGELS

'I have recently been reading about Angels and have asked for their help and guidance on several occasions. One weekend we were going on a camping trip and before we set off I asked the angel of protection to please go before us and prepare our way, and to look after us on our journey.

We'd recently purchased our car and this was our first long journey in it. We travelled down motorways and major roads and through countryside over cattle grids, and eventually we arrived at our destination safe and sound.

After a very enjoyable two days we set off on our return journey, and again I asked the angel of protection to prepare our way and look after us on our journey home. We followed someone home who took us over the hills and round windy paths with great big drops at the side of us. My sons *thought this was fantastic but I was extremely nervous driving with a drop so close by!*

We arrived home safe and sound and I took my car into the garage for its regular safety check and service, and was astounded when my mechanic told me how bad my tyres were! He couldn't believe it and told me that three of my tyres were virtually bald and one of them had a metal wire sticking out of the side. Even worse, one of them had a great big hole in it!

When I told him that we had been travelling on motorways and had covered over 165 miles over the weekend he was shocked. He said that the tyre should have blown months ago and that we were all lucky to be alive!

Lucky or was it the angels? We were definitely protected that weekend!'

Andrea called on the 'angels of protection'. It's useful to use a general term like this because it gives the angels permission to bring in whoever is needed to get the job done! The Archangel Michael is chief of the heavenly armies and can bring in his entire force to protect us. Imagine this great choir of angels surrounding you and your family wherever you go.

> *'When Jesus is corporally present within us,*
> *the angels surround us as a guard of love.'*
> SAINT BERNARD

Using visualization

Use your creative visualization skills to 'see' your angels surrounding you and your family in your mind's eye (your imagination). This strengthens the psychic bond between you and the angelic realms. Believe it as if it had already happened … and so it will.

Here is a list of the angels who look after these particular roles but, like Andrea, you can use the 'angels of protection' as a general term and know that the right angels will appear.

Angels of Protection

Archangel Ariel – Protection outdoors

Archangel Azrael – Protection at sea

Archangel Chamuel – A general angel 'bouncer'

Archangel Gabriel – Protection from vicious words

Archangel Haniel – Psychic protection

Archangel Jeremiel – Protection during major life changes

Archangel Michael – All sorts of protection (particularly physical)

Archangel Raguel – Protection in law and legal matters

Archangel Raphael – Health and healing protection

Archangel Sandalphon – Watches over children and unborn babies

Archangel Sariel – Another angel who watches over children

Archangel Uriel – General Earth protection and healing

Archangel Zadkiel – Emotional protection and spiritual health

♥   ♥   ♥

'Now cracks a noble heart. Good night, sweet prince,
And flights of angels sing thee to thy rest!'

WILLIAM SHAKESPEARE, HAMLET

A *veil of protection*

Have you ever seen an aura photograph? These machines take a photograph of you surrounded by a coloured representation of your energy field. We know we are surrounded by an electrical field and this is now measurable scientifically. This clever photograph shows the different emotions contained within the energy and shows them as different colours. This energy surrounds us all the time and we can make ourselves more aware of the information that it collects around us.

We are very sensitive to energy around us and, like dogs, whose hackles rise when a scary stranger appears, we too react in a physical way when we feel danger around us. When we are scared or in danger, the hairs on our arms will often stand up too!

I don't know about you, but there are times when I have taken an instant dislike to someone without any idea why! I'm not usually wrong, though, and later when I get to know the person

I realize why. The same is true with people of a good heart. We pick up on their energy which intermingles with our own. We 'feel' their personality in this way.

We also do the same thing with buildings and places that we visit. We might walk into a room and say, 'What a lovely room, it feels so cosy and comfortable'. We might also walk into a room where people have recently argued. Even if they have smiles on their faces we can 'feel' the tension in the atmosphere around us. We might say, 'You could cut the air with a knife in here!' or 'Wow – something going on in THAT room!'

Our ability to pick up messages using our energy 'body' is part of our natural protection and instinct and animals use this ability all the time. We might call it our 'psychic' ability because we have difficulty in explaining or classifying this natural ability, but we can learn to develop it and use it to our advantage.

When we feel unhappy or under attack from others this might show up in our energy field as dark areas, and our natural smooth 'egg-shaped' aura appears ragged at the edges. By using our 'imagination' (the power of the mind) we can strengthen and re-build these areas – literally recreate missing areas. Confident and strong people have strong auras and are less easily affected by negative things that happen around them.

Ask your angels to help strengthen your aura, and so your natural instinct in turn becomes stronger. Instincts, after all, save lives.

Building your own protection

You can top up your own protection at any time, and any-where. You might find it easier to close your eyes. Imagine your aura, your energy field surrounding your body. 'See' a cloud of shining light surrounding your whole body. 'Visualize' your energy as having the ability of 'letting in' loving and positive energy from outside sources whilst repelling and rejecting negative and uncomfortable energies. Ask your angels to help seal and strengthen your aura.

Women in particular can also call on the magical Archangel Haniel to help strengthen the aura during fluctuations of hormones. Haniel is the Archangel of the moon and works with women's natural cycles.

4
love and laughter

'... the angel said, "I have learned that every man lives,
not through care of himself, but by love."'

LEO TOLSTOY

Love ...

What is a little angel love? One lady found deep inner peace in a
shop selling angel figurines and said that she would never forget
the feelings of joy she had when opening the door to the shop.

It was so obvious and so beautiful! She said she could feel the angels really liked being in this shop and it was like they belonged there. She felt that the owners must have had a wonderful relationship with angels! Unbelievably, this lady felt that it was the most obvious feeling of angel joy that she'd ever known or felt.

Can a shop be full of angels? We all find peace and joy in different places. For some it will be in a place of worship and for others it will be that special place down by the river or perhaps a cliff top overlooking the sea.

Wherever you find that inner peace the angels will find you. You know that feeling when your heart really opens up? When you go on holiday and walk out onto your hotel balcony on that first night and you take a deep breath and do that huge sigh? When you walk onto a beach with miles of sand? When you climb to the top of a mountain or when you look out over a perfect, still lake? That's the feeling, and that is where we all want to be!

Angels can also offer a helping hand with the simple things in life. If you don't ask, you will never know how they might help you. Go and find your inner 'angel space'.

Angels help with all sorts of tasks, both big and small. It's often the little things which can make the biggest difference. After a workshop I'd taken in Wales, I received the following e-mail:

A LITTLE ANGEL WEIGHT LIFTING

'I haven't tried contacting any angels since the workshop, but my friend who was with me has. She told me that yesterday she went food shopping and bought far too much. It was much more than she could carry alone and way too heavy.

My friend doesn't drive and really struggled to get all the shopping on the bus. She was worried about how she was going to manage to carry it all home as she was now very tired.

> My friend remembered what you had said about the angels so she decided to ask for their help, "Come on angels, please can you do something to help me with my shopping?"
>
> Rather coincidentally, as she dragged all the heavy shopping off the bus, her neighbour turned up unexpectedly with her car and drove her home!'

Shopping angels then! Brilliant!

Sometimes the 'Angels' are our loved ones on the other side … as in this story.

CHRISTINE'S STORY

'My grandmother Barbara and my grandfather loved to take my sister and me to the Magic Kingdom Park in Orlando, Florida, each year when we were very young. It became something we would look forward to annually and sort of became a tradition in a sense.

Over the years my grandmother developed leukaemia and was unable to make our trips any longer. My family and I actually ended up moving to Florida, but I was lucky enough to see her about twice a year whether she was in a hospital bed or her own.

Our relationship was very strong and the struggle weighed heavily on us both. Eventually, she passed over in October of 1999. In December of the same year some girlfriends and I decided to plan a trip up to Orlando and made sure to stop *at the Magic Kingdom one evening. My grandmother was in the back of my mind the entire trip, but the memories were happy so I decided not to let them bother me.*

When our Disney appetite had been fulfilled we made the customary stop at one of the stores to get our last minute, unnecessary souvenirs. My friend Lauren and I were thinking about buying a little ring or necklace so we were standing at one of the jewellery displays browsing. The four-sided display carousel had rings on one side, nameplates on another, and the last two had anklets and bracelets. I couldn't find my name in the nameplates so I settled for a ring.

Lauren tried to help me find one I would like when she noticed that a nameplate was misplaced with the rings and it read my name! This was strange and we both said, "Weird", but we kept on looking just the same. As I looked down, though, I realized that one more nameplate (but just these

two), *was also misplaced and hanging with the rings. It read*
"Grandma".

*The sheer coincidence of the event was enough for me to
know that she was saying hello and that she had the same
fond memories of us in this special place. It's something that
I will never forget and the reason that I believe that there is a
place for beautiful souls to rest and watch over us.'*

Janet Pearson is from Canada. She had a mystery Valentine for
years before she discovered their secret …

HAPPY VALENTINE

All the way through her twenties and early thirties, Janet had a secret admirer. Her admirer sent Janet an anonymous gift every single Valentine's Day for years and years. Try as she might, Janet couldn't guess the sender of the yearly gift. She and her friend Kelly had a lot of fun talking about who the mystery man might be.

As fate would have it, Kelly developed cancer and died on the Summer Solstice, June 21, still a young woman. The following February 14th, Valentine's Day, Janet received a package. It was Kelly's mother sending Janet a box of Kelly's belongings. This was when Janet discovered the identity of her secret admirer. After all those years, it had been her best friend Kelly!

... *and Laughter*

I did a little search on the internet to see if I could find some jokes on angels that I might share with you, but the joke was on me! All I could find was rude jokes about angels but it didn't matter, I found some true-life funny angel stories instead. But I'll start with my own!

Did you know that angels have a sense of humour? Well, mine do! As well as an author, I am a columnist, feature writer, angel teacher and owner of an online shop. I am a pretty busy person and I was feeling a little stressed when I remembered that I had not prepared for a workshop I had planned the next day. I like to feed my guests something special when they attend my workshops, but I'm not a cook!

It was late into the evening and my only hope was to call at my local 24-hour supermarket. I jumped into the car and cursed when I had only driven a mile from home and my mobile telephone rang. The phone played out its usual tune (Robbie Williams' song 'Angels'; what else!) but it was only my daughter calling. She had wanted to come shopping with me to buy chocolate! I was in a hurry so promised to bring some home with me rather than drive home to get her.

I was still cursing my forgetfulness when the telephone rang again a few moments later. Carefully, I pulled the car over to a lay-by to answer the phone again. This time I was really cross. I snatched up the phone and clicked the green button.

'Yes?' I answered moodily. 'Hello?'

But no one was there and rather bizarrely the phone continued to ring. I gave the phone a shake and pressed the green button again. The phone still rang but this time it seemed like the sound might be coming from the back of the car. You guessed it – I climbed into the back of the car! Now the sound was coming from the front of the car so I climbed back into the front. The 'Angels' tune continued to play and I felt a little silly.

What was going on? I sat and pondered. No one else in the family had a phone which played the same tune as my phone. In fact I knew no one who had that particular tune at all. It had to be my phone that was ringing. I picked up the phone again to see if there was a caller number on the front. Nothing. Was there a number recorded on the last number section? No, that wasn't it. Was the sound turned up or down? No.

Was I going crazy? I checked the car radio and then the CD player. I couldn't think of anything else but I could still hear the tune play. I continued my drive and shortly the supermarket was in sight, and as I pulled into my parking space I switched off the engine. The music stopped immediately and I burst out laughing. I was being grumpy but it was my own fault – disorganized as usual. I think the angels were saying, 'Thanks for doing this just the same!' And just to make sure that my bad mood hadn't affected my driving skills I think they drove with me all the way there.

Now you know what is really strange? During my research for this book I discovered an extraordinary 'coincidence'. In an internet forum, someone else who works with angels had written, '... When I am booked to do an Angel Card party, either on the way there or on the way home again Robbie Williams ALWAYS comes on the car radio singing "Angels". It's our little joke!'

I think this 'little joke' works for many of us! Do we take life too seriously? I think we do. It is hard to forget that we are spiritual beings having a human experience. It's important to remember that life is a big wonderful game.

Nick Richardson, the Cornish writer and columnist, dedicates much of his work to writing about the humorous side of our lives as spiritual beings, and he urges us to laugh at ourselves more. I believe the angels agree with him. Humour is an important learning tool.

> '*I have just started to connect with my angel and it has*
> *made me feel good about life …*'
>
> MAUREEN

I asked my angel friends if they thought angels had a sense of humour and my friend Glennyce Eckersley (author of *An Angel at my Shoulder*) told me a funny story from one of her workshops:

ANGELS WITH A SENSE OF HUMOUR

'*When speaking at a workshop some time ago, a lady asked if I thought angels had a sense of humour. Before I could reply, another lady stood up and said they certainly did. She had been searching for a new spiritual path and, having tried several things, she felt let down. She saw an advertisement for a weekend to learn Reiki healing and felt very drawn to it. Booking herself in, she grew more and more convinced that this was to be a wise choice.*

The day arrived and, driving to the venue, she felt sure the angels were guiding her. Suddenly there was a white feather stuck to the windscreen; it appeared from nowhere it seemed. Thrilled, she felt her heart sing, "The angels have confirmed that I am on my correct spiritual path," she thought.

A little further along the road another white feather stuck to the windscreen, this time she was ecstatic! A wonderful gift from the angels. Turning left at the next junction, however, she saw immediately in front of her a lorry load of chickens, flapping about and feathers flying in all directions!

"That will teach me," she laughed, "the angels are having a good chuckle at my expense."'

Angels can also create fun experiences in our lives. Jill Wellington is the American author of *Fireworks* (a spiritual novel which includes the introduction of a spiritual guide to the plot).

AN ANGEL'S SPECIAL TREAT

Jill remembers an early encounter of her own when an angel helped her as a four year old. She recalls standing outside a neighbour's house when the ice cream truck rounded the corner, its lively music attracting children like ants. Jill was sad because she had no money for an ice cream and watched as the other kids gathered around the colourful truck.

Jill's spiritual guardian obviously felt sorry for the young child and she recalls an idea popping into her head … 'Go to the garden.' She moved over to the garden and dropped to her knees. Half buried in the soil was a shiny coin, exactly enough money to buy an ice cream cone!

Jill has had many experiences with her angels since that day and the encounter has influenced her work ever since. Jill is also a very successful writer and journalist and credits her spiritual guides and guardian angels with their help in her work.

She still cherishes her ice-cream memory, and knows her guardian angel treated her to an ice cream cone on that special day.

Not all problems seem important, but everyone's problems are important to them. Angels appreciate this and are listening to you. No problem is too big or too small so give it a try! Ask your angels for their help.

Be open to communication in your inner ear. Be ready for their messages to arrive in many ways that are not related to our own limited language!

> *'The angels are so enamoured of the language that is spoken in heaven that they will not distort their lips with the hissing and unmusical dialects of men, but speak their own, whether there be any who understand it or not.'*
>
> RALPH WALDO EMERSON

No job is too small for angels and it seems they can turn their hand to more or less anything. One lady wrote:

AN ANGEL'S COWBOY CRAFTS

'*I remember very clearly the time my son was a cowboy in his Kindergarten Circus. Markey needed a cowboy hat and I did not want to invest a lot of money when he would wear it just this one time.*

I looked around the hobby shops for a cheap cowboy hat, but found nothing. I was beginning to panic when one night I had a vivid dream. I saw a stage with a heavy velvet curtain. An angel's voice said, "I am going to show you how to make a cowboy hat!" The curtain opened and I saw a cowboy hat made out of black cardboard, strung together with twine! I saw it for only a few seconds, but immediately knew exactly how to make it.

I jumped out of bed and found some black poster board and some twine. I made the hat and it looked just like the

> *one in my dream! It wasn't the best hat among the cowboys in his class, but it was the most special!'*

I agree! And it was made with the love of the angels too! Now this next story is in a class of its own! I don't even know what to call it! It's definitely one of the funniest angel stories that I have read!

ANGELS FOR 'ALL' EMERGENCIES!

'My mother's friends were out for a Sunday afternoon drive and decided to go see the big houses in the new neighbour-hood. After enjoying the splendid homes, Richard had to go to the bathroom NOW!

> They rounded a corner and there was a portable toilet in a yard right by the road. Richard jumped out and used it. Thank goodness – it almost looked as if it had been placed there especially for him.
>
> Relieved, he jumped back into the car, but both Richard and his wife commented on how unusual it was to find the portable toilet, especially since the construction of new properties was complete in the area. They went around the block and the toilet was no longer there! They were astounded and figured an angel was having a good laugh!'

Angels take their work with us seriously, but they're not against having fun. Enjoy their humorous ways!

5

humans or angels?

'...but we all are men, in our own natures frail,

and capable of our flesh;

few are angels …'

WILLIAM SHAKESPEARE, *KING HENRY VIII*

Humans or angels? Sometimes it's hard for us to tell the difference. Children see things most clearly and have their own specific ideas about what an angel is and isn't. I asked a few junior experts their opinions:

What children say

Dakota (age two) says that angels are pink shiny people!

Maya Rose (age three) says angels come to her at night while she is sleeping and look to see if she has cleaned her teeth. Apparently, they always check to see if her hands and face have been washed before going to bed. Maya Rose says that all children have their own angel looking after them.

Cierra (age four) says that angels fly and they come down and visit you when you are sad so they can make you smile and happy inside.

Shania (age four) says that angels help look after all the little children when they are sleeping.

Jade (age four) says an angel is a Christmas thing and her name is Woopsy Daisy.

Benjie (age five) 'I have two angels. One sleeps with me and makes sure nothing bad happens to me and my other angel plays with me and watches everything I do. My angel is very big and strong and his face shines like a light.' His mother says, 'This is a boy who I believe has seen angels since he was a little one. I remember him playing and laughing as if he was with someone when in fact he was playing alone.'

Angharad (age six) 'An angel is like a fairy. They fly about at night.'

Brandon (age seven) says an angel is a piece of air '… when people die they go to heaven and become an angel and they are there to sing songs.'

Angelica (age seven), known by the family as 'Angel': 'I think an angel is my shadow, it is always behind me making sure I am safe.'

Rhiannon (age eight) 'I think an angel is a thing that flutters around watching us. I think an angel is a lovely creature. I like angels – I love them!'

Bradley (age eight) told his Grandma (Grana) that she was his angel!

Mark (age eight) 'I think an angel is someone who's nice and helpful and you can trust them. They live in Heaven.'

Emma (age eight) 'I think angels are very pretty people and they help lots of people with things. I imagine them flying about with their haloes on top of their heads and little, small dresses on them. I imagine them blonde haired and very small.'

Allisha (age eleven) says that an angel is there in heaven and they guide you when you have a problem.

Will (age twelve) says an angel is a protector, a guardian, and someone that helps you. He says that after he'd had open heart surgery at three years old, a beautiful angel with long blonde hair told him that it was time to go back home to his mummy, and he has seen angels ever since. 'I know they are always there when I need them and all I have to do is call to them and they appear.'

Steve (age thirteen) says an angel is someone who's been sent here to help out.

Nicolle (age thirteen) believes that angels are here to guide, help and protect us. 'They are around us all the time. There are even some people that can see and feel them. Even though they are not visible to me, I know they are there to help guide and protect me.'

One little girl saw a tall lady in a long white dress. She said that the 'lady' was very pretty with long hair and had just a few feathers on her arms.

Adults, too, have their thoughts on these spiritual beings. I wanted to know people's thoughts and feeling about them.

What adults say

'My angels have created miracles in so many ways in my life like a new job, a new life, a new apartment that is incredible. They always find a way to let me know they are here with me and send love to me in some special way … They guide and protect me.'

Donna is an actress from Birmingham. She says, '… an angel is the hope, faith and friend that gives me the strength to achieve each day.'

Len is a factory worker from Bristol and says: 'An angel to me is my helper when I heal, and my confidante and support when I have need.'

Paula is retired and lives in Derbyshire. She says: 'An angel is simply a comfort; I know my angel is with me day and night, and I am safe knowing this.'

Gail from Barnet is a Corporate Administrator and she says, 'My angel has made me realize that life is worth living even though she is no longer with me in body – her spirit is always going to be here with me – and that is what keeps me going.'

Humans as 'angels'?

In a recent internet poll, visitors were asked if they believed that their loved ones become angels after death. The highest percentage (56%) felt that they did, with 29% saying no, and 13% voting that they weren't sure.

Angels regularly appear as people ('human beings'), and not until medieval times did we begin to see angels with halos. Early angels were not seen with wings either, and accounts differ as to why angels might need them. Earlier cultures believed that angels would need wings to fly although many people felt that angels appeared with wings in artwork to distinguish them from the humans around them! Perhaps now, angels appear to us with wings because that is what we expect of them! So, we see what we think we are going to see.

The early church had difficulty with this question and had to decide if angels were pure spirit or corporeal. Although the scriptures say that angels do appear as men it also uses the word *spiritus* (Hebrews 1:14) to describe them. Early people were beginning to worship angels, which was also a problem for the church, as this went against God being the only true leader. Many people found the idea of angels as human-like figures easier to understand.

Throughout the Middle Ages, angels continued to be a hot topic for debate, with even serious scholars debating whether angels were men or beings of light.

Angels as loved ones from the afterlife

There is much confusion on this topic as more and more of our loved ones come back in 'visitation' to pass on messages of love and support from the other side. Here is another story which illustrates this.

Lesley's young daughter seems aware of her older brother who appears to be watching and supporting his family from the other side. Is he an 'angel?'

HELLO MUM

'I lost my eighteen-year-old son on the 24th August 2004 and I have a little girl who is now 21 months, who has shown the most incredible understanding of the situation.

From the beginning, if she looks into my eyes, even when I have not been crying but I am feeling a lot of pain inside, she says, "It's all right, mummy," and hugs me. Sometimes, she will stare into my eyes for the longest time and turn my head back to face her, especially if I look away after a couple of minutes because I am going to cry.

Last week I put her in her car seat and when I got into the driver's side she said to me, "Mum, I see Ryan."

When I asked her, "Where is he?" she told me he said, "Hello."

> *I have been amazed at how perceptive she has been so far in this horrible situation and there is no way that at her age I would have thought that she is capable of making up the fact that she saw him.*
>
> *If she had been older and we had been discussing Ryan before we went into the car then maybe she could have invented a story which would have been quite normal at three or four years old, but my instinct is telling me there is more to this!'*

Elaine was surprised by her kitchen visitors. I was honoured that she gave permission for me to use her story here.

HAPPY BIRTHDAY!

'It was the morning of my fortieth birthday and as usual I wandered downstairs to turn the alarm off and put the kettle on! It was early and I shuffled down the corridor to the kitchen. As I opened the door to the kitchen I was met by the most beautiful image of three 'angels' with their arms outstretched as if to hug me.

I cannot describe to you the overwhelming feeling of love and warmth that literally overcame me. The brightness, the love ... this experience was over far too quickly. For the longest time afterwards, I was in tears and could hardly explain to my husband what had just happened to me.

My mother had died ten years before, and her mum and my aunt before that; all of them with cancer and all of *us very close. I knew it was them, but have only told my story to a handful of people that I know will understand.*

This was a very important morning in my life and one that I hope will be repeated. I have had many more experiences since then that have strengthened my beliefs in the afterlife and my angels on the other side.'

Living human angels

On many occasions, angels come to us in the form of a human being. Sometimes we are unsure if we are encountering real-life angels or humans given to us to play the part of an angel on earth … or are they? Who was this stranger who disappeared into the night?

PROTECTED IN THE CAB

'*I drive a cab in Norfolk, Virginia, on the night shift. I had picked up a young man at a local store. He was going to Hampton which is a $37 fare (flat rate, out of town) at about 1.45 am. He was wearing baggy jeans and an oversized football jersey. I explained to him that he had to pay in advance when going out of town at that time of night. He* *handed me a fifty and I gave him his change so there didn't seem to be an immediate problem.*

About half way there I began to get nervous. Rather unusually he seemed very quiet and I couldn't get him talking at all. As I got off the interstate I began looking for a patrol car but couldn't see one anywhere. My passenger had me drive into a dark, quiet street and the house we pulled up outside appeared deserted. All the while I was praying for a patrol car to turn up because I felt so uncomfortable about the whole situation.

Just at that moment, my passenger lifted up his shirt with his left hand and began reaching across to his waistband with his right. I knew what was coming. As I flipped on the interior light I could see his gun clearly.

All of a sudden I noticed a change of expression cross his face. His eyes were as wide as saucers, and his lower jaw was agape. I looked to my left and saw a police car had pulled to a stop right next to me! My side window was part way down but there was no sound from that car's engine, no sound of tyres on the pavement and no glimpse of approaching headlights … nothing! The guy started stammering and asked me what he owed me! I reminded him that he had already paid me so he quickly walked off.

I couldn't believe it and as I turned my head to thank the patrol car for stopping and to explain what had happened, the patrol car had gone and I never even heard it pull away! I drove all around the area and I never did find them! I never even saw headlights or tail lights in the distance anywhere!

Whoever, or whatever it was that stopped next to my cab quite possibly saved my life that night. All I could do was thank God all the way back home.

A long time ago, a dear friend in Texas said he asked for a guardian angel to watch over me when I'm out working and I think he drives a heavenly police car! Any other explanation? I sure can't think of one!'

Maybe we should all ask for our angels to sit with us when we drive!

Lynne's story is very bizarre indeed. We are certainly left with the questions, 'who was that?' and 'How did he know?'

AN ANGEL ESCORT

'Shortly after my father died I took an overdose. I was just
16 years old. I was taken to the hospital but they didn't
pump my stomach. I walked from the hospital and immediately went to the train station to catch my train home.

Whilst I was unconscious, most of my money had been
stolen and I only had enough train fare to get home, but I
realized that I'd missed the last train. I hadn't realized that
I was in a red light area and sat down on the side of the
pavement. I think the tablets had started to take effect, and
when a man approached me as if from nowhere I naturally
became scared. I challenged him and he calmed me down
and said he was only coming to see if I was all right. I
explained to the stranger that my money had been taken
and he told me that he was a long-distance lorry driver and

was just about to call a taxi to take him back to work. He asked me if I wanted to share his taxi. I was a little worried but felt I had no other option.

The taxi appeared suddenly and we both got in. On the way he told me his name was Melvin and he actually said to me, "Why did you take the tablets, Lynne?" I was slightly spooked because and I hadn't told him my name and I hadn't told him about the overdose either.

The stranger felt safe, though, so I happily talked to him. When we arrived at his depot, he got out and paid the driver, instructing him to drive me back to my town. As soon as I arrived home I was taken straight back to the hospital.

The following day I got a phone call from Melvin, making sure I was all right. I've never forgotten him even though he never contacted me again after that.

If he wasn't an angel from heaven then he was one from

> *earth. He knew what I had done, he knew my phone number and he appeared out of nowhere just as I needed someone.'*

Sometimes it is more obvious that the helper is a human being. But did the angels help here? Sue is one of the hundreds of people who've attended one of my workshops. Several months later, she e-mailed me her own amazing story.

THE ANGELS OF PRETTY MUCH EVERYTHING!

'The week before Christmas I was in a really bad car accident, where my car rolled into a field and landed upside down. Since meeting you I now ask Archangel Michael for protection before I or any of my family go out. I came out of that accident with just a bruised ankle! Now if you'd seen the car you'd have thought that no one could have survived.

The following evening I was feeling particularly sorry for myself as my life hadn't been going well for a couple of years. As a single mum of three children, I run my own business. Christmas is my busiest time of year, and the accident had made me lose my Christmas trade as well.

I decided to settle myself down, watch a film and get the place nice and cosy and relaxing by burning a few candles and warming up the house. But as I turned the switch on my central heating, nothing happened at all! Well, that was just it! I completely dissolved into a crying fit. What was I to do, how on earth was I going to afford a new heating system? I just knew that the whole thing would need replacing because it was so ancient. In my despair I decided to ask my angels to help me to sort this one out, and just went to bed with a hot water bottle.

I nearly passed out the next morning when I opened my post. A huge brown envelope (which I felt sure was a tax bill) was sitting on the mat. In huge letters the first words on the letter were "STEP OUT OF THE COLD … you as a single parent are entitled to a heating grant for £1,500!" These angels act fast.

I can't get over it, and really don't believe that could have been a coincidence. The angels are with me and support me always. I know they are by my side and with their help I can get through anything.'

Emanuel Swedenborg – the man who chatted to angels

Emanuel Swedenborg was born in 1688. Many people call him the Leonardo da Vinci of his era. As a young man he studied science and he was the leading mathematician in Sweden. He was an amazing linguist who spoke nine languages. He was a politician and a businessman who turned his hand to many things including engraving and astronomy. He even wrote books on such things as metallurgy, colour theory, commerce, economics, physics and chemistry among other things! Swedenborg was also an inventor.

He was a very spiritual person and meditated regularly. With experience he learnt how to enter deep trances and left his physical body to visit heavenly realms. Swedenborg talked to angels and spirits and his work is well respected even today. He was permitted exclusive insights into heaven and was shown firsthand the arrival of newly deceased spirits, as they were shown a review of the life they had recently left. Swedenborg called this 'the opening of the Book of Lives'. This is the experience which many people recount during a near death experience when they say that their lives 'passed before their eyes'.

He explained how the information that arose during the opening of the Book of Lives was recorded within the person's spiritual body. Swedenborg says that the angels were able to understand this information by 'reading' the spiritual body of the deceased spirit.

His fascinating accounts describe how the angels communicated using holographic thought balls to send telepathic bursts of knowledge as a picture language so dense with information that each image contained a thousand ideas. These communications were said to last for many hours.

He suggests that angels can use a type of speech which is really beyond our understanding but they use this because it is the only way they can even begin to communicate in a way that we might understand.

Swedenborg's understanding has to be seen through the eyes of someone living in his time, but there is no reason why his experiences can't be built upon today.

He has inspired generations of people with his visions and fifteen years after his death a church denomination named after him was formed in London. Later, the Swedenborgian Church in North America was created (early 1800s). Although we really know very little about angels, Swedenborg, it seems, knew more than most.

If you want more information about Swedenborg and his work, visit the Swedenborg Society (UK), a registered charity:

http://www.swedenborg.org.uk/ which publishes books and gives talks about his work. The society also has a large library of his works. Try also the Swedenborg Foundation (US): http://www.swedenborg.com. A quick internet search will enable you to find many other websites.

angels — who are they really?

'Angels are spirits, but it is not because they are spirits that they are angels. They become Angels when they are sent. For the name Angel refers to their office, not their nature. You ask the name of this nature, it is spirit; you ask its office, it is that of an Angel, which is a messenger.'

SAINT AUGUSTINE

Is it an angel?

What makes an experience an angelic encounter? Perhaps there is no defining scientific explanation and it's all down to personal perception. Have you ever asked an angel to show you they are around? Give it a try and then you too might be amazed at what happens to you! Expect the unexpected!

> *'Angels are speaking to all of us …*
> *some of us are only listening better …'*
> **ANONYMOUS**

Many people feel confident enough to ask an angel to help them to find a parking space or to help look after their loved ones, but angels can do so much more. As long as you distinguish between asking them to help you complete a task and expecting them to take over the job for you, then there isn't a problem!

An angel's role is not to live our lives, after all. What point would there be in coming to earth to have another being make every decision. Angels work best when they help us to help ourselves. Ask your angels to help you find your own path and even to hold your hand along the way. That is the role of an angel.

> *'As long as you are asking for help, you might*
> *as well ask for help from the universe. You never*
> *know what might happen.'*
> ELAINE SAINT JAMES, *INNER SIMPLICITY*

What do we call them?

In medieval times, thousands of angels were literally 'made up' by adding 'el' and 'irion' to the end of Hebrew nouns. Before long there were all these extra 'angels' who had never existed before. Pretending angels?

Another way that extra angels appeared from nowhere was when foreign gods' names were 'borrowed' and the letters 'el' added to the end. So now you know!

There are many hundreds more angel names which are passed on through generation to generation and others which appear in religious texts and in fables and legends. Each guardian angel has its own task or role, but how does this work in practice?

In the heavenly realms, the angel names are not really relevant in the way that they are on the earth plane. Naming things is a very human thing to do and we also like to categorize even the very holiest of things.

Angels are a 'light' vibration – not something which needs a name, really. Angels are celestial beings whose role is LOVE. Everything they do is in this role. They are love, they give love.

Many of their names come from the role that they play, with the addition of the phrase 'of the lord', or 'of God', which pretty well sums up most of them. Basically, humans make up the angel names!

Here is a list of the most commonly known archangels:

Archangel Ariel – Lion of God

Archangel Azrael – Whom God helps

Archangel Chamuel – He who sees God

Archangel Gabriel – Power of God

Archangel Haniel – Glory of God

Archangel Jeremiel – Mercy of God

Archangel Jophiel – Beauty of God

Archangel Metatron – Adjacent to God

Archangel Michael – Looks like God

Archangel Raguel – Friend of God

Archangel Raphael – God heals

Archangel Raziel – Secrets of God

Archangel Sandalphon – God's Prayers

Archangel Uriel – Light of God

Archangel Zadkiel – Righteousness of God

When do we call them?

The above list includes many of the archangels who are working on our planet at this moment. They are some of our 'Earth Angels', and we can call upon them for assistance.

Archangel Michael is probably the best known. Pictured mainly with his flaming sword of protection, he stands guard over people in need. Archangel Gabriel is the angel of communication and can be called upon to help us with messages of importance; even with our modern communication systems. You could call the Archangel Gabriel to assist you with calls on your mobile phone or using your laptop computer, just as easily as you would have asked for help with writing a letter in the past. Angels are moving with the times!

You do not need to know the intricacies of which archangel does which task. They have many more roles than we can even begin to fathom. Just ask your angels for help and the right one will come along at the right time.

Our own personal helpers and guardians will sometimes give us their name in visions and dreams, but it doesn't have to come to you as some magical or tropical sounding name. If you want a name for your own helper then you can always ask for one to come to you. Does it matter if it's wrong? No. There is no such thing as wrong. If a name feels right to you then use that.

The extent of their role

Angels are not babysitters. Think of them more as trainers. Imagine your own guardian angel as being your personal coach. Your angel may feel it would be useful for you to train for that big race at least 4 days a week and suggest you get out of bed to attend practice. If you don't turn up for a session then it's not the angel's fault … you have to take on some of the responsibility for yourself. They nurture your skills and then, when the time comes for that final race (or races) your angels are there standing on the sidelines cheering you on. If you win, then the angels are thrilled for you and jump up and down in excitement, but if you lose, they stand with their hands on your shoulder in support and help you to achieve your goals better the next time.

'*It must be affirmed that angels and everything existing,*
except God, were made by God.'
SUMMA THEOLOGICA, THOMAS AQUINAS (1225–1274)

There is no judgement from your guardians. Yet at the same time
they cannot run that race for you, for if they did, then to whom
should the winner's cup go? You, or your angels? We are the ones
who have to do the work, but their support is always there. In
this journey of life, we need to plan our own goals but there is no
need to work alone. Our unseen helpers are always at the ready,
waiting to be asked for their help.

Imagine that you are specializing in a particular area, maybe
track racing, and you ask your angels for help. All of a sudden,
your coach meets another trainer who can give you extra classes
on a Saturday morning to assist with this specialized skill. Your
own coach can set up this extra lesson for you. Alternatively, if
you want to diversify into other areas, then you can request

extra help whenever you wish. Your own guardian angels can help to make this happen for you. Whatever you want to do with your own life, ask the angels to assist you. They can certainly make things a lot easier!

Your guardian angels and spiritual guides can help to place the perfect person into your life at the right time … as if by coincidence! Ask – then start working towards your goals. Keep talking to other people about your needs. Maybe their angels will prompt them to be at the ready. You will probably find yourself asking the one person you need to assist you!

> *'Somehow the Angels comfort me whenever I have tears*
> *And always they encourage me to overcome my fears …'*
>
> MARTINA TARANDEK, 'ANGELS' PRAYER'

What can they do?

Ask angels to help you do better at the things you want to do.
They can:

- ♥ Help with protection
- ♥ Assist with personal study and learning
- ♥ Aid us with communication skills
- ♥ Place helpful people in front of us
- ♥ Help us to be in the right place at the right time
- ♥ Get us to the right place at the right time
- ♥ Help us to find useful information
- ♥ Calm us
- ♥ Comfort us

- ♥ Heal us
- ♥ Assist us in creating and exploring our natural skills
- ♥ Inspire us to help others
- ♥ Encourage us to assist people, pets and even our planet in times of danger
- ♥ Help us to explore and stretch our own boundaries
- ♥ Aid our personal development and growth as human souls
- ♥ Walk with us on life's journey

'How do you know if an angel has crossed your path?
Sometimes you don't, because angels often appear
as coincidences. That is, they seem like chance events,
but they are really part of God's carefully orchestrated
plan for your life.'
GARY KINNAMAN, ANGELS DARK AND LIGHT

Where do angels come from? Where do they live? Do they spend their time in heaven, only to visit us when we call? Many say we will never know until we start our new heavenly life.

'It is not known precisely where angels dwell – whether
in the air, the void, or the planets. It has not been God's
pleasure that we should be informed of their abode.'

VOLTAIRE

Ideas for ways that your angels can help you

Career

Are you frustrated with your work? Are you ready for a change? Then your angels can assist you. Ask your angels to help you, but write down a few notes first of all so you can be clear in your mind about what it is you want. For example, are you looking for a change of career or a promotion in the job you are in now?

Angels can assist by bringing you clarity in seeing which direction to take next. Look out for people who talk about areas which interest you, TV programmes which stir your interest or leaflets about training which might drop through your letter box.

Archangels Haniel and Uriel can assist with learning new skills and working on interviews.

Here is a story of how one woman's angel helped support a change in career direction.

A CAREER ANGEL

'I am on an "Angelic journey", and have been learning and experiencing a lot. I hear voices, see messages, and see angelic spheres of light. I talk to my angels all of the time. For the last two years I've had an angel with me. Her name is Arah. I don't see her or hear her, but she helps guide me through my thoughts and intuition.

Arah arrived not as a voice or a vision, but in thoughts and guided drawing. I was at home one evening, contemplating how I could change my career as well as my life. As usual I worried about it and was feeling quite low. After I had played some relaxing music I lit my candles. For some reason I had this overwhelming feeling that I should get out my sketch book. I started drawing a face then hair, a dress and some wings. Wings?

Even I was surprised. I had never been interested in drawing angels before. In the hands of the angel was an ornate bottle, and in my mind's eye I was imagining it filled with perfume or oils (although my basic drawing skills weren't able to capture the angel's elaborate details in the way I had seen them in my mind).

Then a word came into my thoughts. I heard the name Arah. I had never heard of such a word but I believed that this was "her" name. It sounded too lovely to mean anything else, so Arah it was and still is.

I have since researched the name, and found it was mentioned in the Dead Sea Scrolls, an angel name meaning "the traveller".

Since then, Arah has guided me towards a more fulfilling career. She is with me supporting me. In the last year I retrained in anatomy and physiology of the human body, and have become qualified in Aromatherapy and blending essential oils. I have started my own company and have developed over 42 blended products (four of which are my Archangel blends).

I now travel to people's houses talking about the benefits of essential oils. I believe that without my angel's intervention, this was something I would have never have even dreamt of doing.'

This next lady's angels seem to have a sense of humour in the way they give their messages! A new job and flowers too – perfect!

LOVELY LILACS

'Once, I was on my way to an interview for a new job. I love lilacs, so I asked my guardian angel to show me lilacs if this job was right for me. During the week leading up to my interview I didn't see any lilacs. I was disappointed, but figured it was late spring and most of the lilacs had already dropped.

As I walked up to the building for my interview, I was suddenly overcome by the strong scent of lilacs! I looked down and saw a lilac bush planted by the door with one single stem of flowers still in bloom. I got the job!'

Finances/Abundance

'*Men ate the bread of angels;*
He sent them all the food they could eat.'
Psalms 78:25

Are you struggling to pay the bills? Are you finding it hard to make ends meet each month? (Do you have too much month left at the end of your money?) Ask the angels to help you find ways of balancing financial flow.

It would be nice to ask your angels for the lotto numbers or the winning bingo numbers. It can happen but it normally doesn't! Angels can help you to find ways of balancing your cash or living within your means. Maybe a move of house or change of direction is needed. Are you paying out for things you no longer use? Can you handle things in a more efficient way? Would it help to be more organized with your bills and paperwork? Sometimes the simplest of things can make the biggest difference to your finances.

Archangel Michael is the one to ask for assistance with financial security. Gabriel and Metatron will assist with any communication skills you need when organizing your finances, like letter writing or telephone calls.

Angels can provide for us in a financial way. Have you ever heard of the saying, 'Follow your bliss', as a way of guiding you on your path? Another favourite saying of mine is, 'Do what you love and the money will follow'. It works for me!

Often there is no one right path or way to live your life. Each choice creates learning and growing experience, so do what makes you feel good, as long as you are not harming others. Following a career which is wrong for you can actually make you ill. I remember doing jobs that I hated in the past and having to take sick leave.

If you get out of bed each day and say, 'Oh no, I can't stand another day in that place', then it's definitely time for a change. Ask yourself, 'How does this work make me feel?' Ask your angels to guide you. A job is only 'work' if it is something you don't like doing. When you are enjoying your career you feel good about yourself and the world around you. You have more energy to live your life. Things around you just work. Ask the angels to help you to live in your own integrity, to be real to yourself. Follow your own dreams – but just ask the angels to help it to happen.

The angels can't fix everything but they can help you to fix things for yourself. They can help empower you to be the best you can be – whatever 'best' is to you. Angels want us to be happy and to rejoice in our lives. Stress can come when we are living our lives to please others. Depression can appear when our lives are out of control or, more correctly, out of our control.

There are some things we can't change, especially those which involve the free will of others. They too have their own path to walk. But there are so many things we can do to direct our own lives. If it's not us at the controls of our own destiny then who is? Do you leave every decision in your life for other people to make on your behalf? Do you look for advice on every move you make?

What makes you happy? What makes you laugh? Walk your walk, follow your dream. Walk your own destiny using your own mind. Take over the wheel and drive along your own road to be 'real', to who you really are.

> *'Since God often sends us inspirations by means of His*
> *angels, we should frequently return our aspirations to him*
> *by means of the same messengers.'*
> **SAINT FRANCIS DE SALES**

An American friend of mine told me a story of a man his family had met. This man had dedicated his life to healing.

THE ANGELS PROVIDE

'The healing man, John, travels from city to city to heal people and told us he doesn't even have a home! He stays with people along the way. He says this is his life's work, and he will continue until he dies.

He barely gets any money (he doesn't charge), but people give love offerings. Once, he was totally broke and stopped at a gas station. A man came up to him and handed him $100 and said, "I don't know why, but I'm supposed to give you this!"

John actually fell to his knees and started crying as he was so overwhelmed with the kindness of this "angel" and the enormity of knowing he will always be provided for!'

Here is another great story about angels helping with money. Theresa remembered to ask for help when things were difficult along her path.

THE PERFECT AMOUNT OF MONEY

'My marriage has been in turmoil for over a year. God has continuously led me to stay in the marriage, even when many times I don't want to. One day I fasted for insight as to what I should do – no one knew that I was fasting. A few weeks prior to this day I awoke feeling that I should go to an "estate sale", which is a sale of a person's estate and personal effects; often the belongings of a deceased person.

After starting my day, I forgot to go, but that evening, my sister called saying that she had just visited the best estate sale she'd ever been to! Immediately, I remembered that *inclination I had felt to go to the estate sale. I asked my sister if it was too late for me to go. She said it was, but maybe we could call the house and try to stop by the next day. This is not a normal occurrence with estate sales. Usually, once they are over, they are over. We called and the daughter of the deceased woman said that we could come over. She was very nice. We took boxes of spiritual and metaphysical books home and also had a nice evening of conversation with the woman and her sister.*

I was slightly confused because I had no idea why the spirit led me to go to this sale in the first place. Both the women that we visited were divorced and had endured similar trials in their marriages to my own so I thought maybe that was a sign for me. Both of them thought they had stayed too long in their marriages.

On the day that I fasted, I was taking my son to the

library. I'd had a conversation that morning with my husband about financial support from him. He told me that although he didn't have much to give me, he prayed for all of us every day. It was somewhat comforting to hear, although I thought he was just trying to get out of assisting us, too.

On the way out to the library, I decided to read one of the many books I had picked up from the estate sale. I went back into my house to grab the book, called A Brush with Angels, *and when I opened it there was a bank envelope inside the cover. Written on the envelope were the month and year of my wedding (11/97) and inside the envelope was $600.*

I took this as confirmation of what the Lord had been telling me – to stay within my marriage – and also that he recognized my fast. The number 600 was important because God had used the number six in other instances in relation to my marriage. Also, I was able to learn the significance of not telling anyone about my fast. Later, he even gave me a scripture that says, in essence, go pray and fast privately and I will reward you openly for it. That is exactly what happened because I told everyone that I knew about the money I found, but because I had said nothing to anyone earlier, I knew that the Lord had heard my prayers.

A few weeks later, still in distress about my marriage, I called a phone line for prayer in tears. The woman who prayed with me stayed on the phone with me because she realized I was very upset. She kept pleading with Christ to give me a sign that He was with me. I calmed down, hung up and went to work. The first thing I saw when reaching my desk was another angel book, and this time with a rainbow on it, which God has also used as a sign for me in the past. It was just a used angel book, but no one to this day at

> *my place of employment has claimed that book or can explain where it came from. It still sits on my desk as a reminder of the angels.'*

There is a postscript to this story, because when I wrote to Theresa to confirm the story many months later she was still struggling with her relationship, and she feels that when she opened my email it reminded her not to give up on her marriage, which still needs healing. She felt she was receiving a spiritual message which reminded her of all the encouragement she had already received along the way.

It does sound as if the angels of love and romance have been helping with this story too. Can they help you with 'a little angel love?'

Love and Romance

> '*For the Lord, the God of heaven, who took me from my*
> *father's house and my native land, solemnly promised to*
> *give this land to my offspring. He will send his angel*
> *ahead of you, and he will see to it that you find a*
> *young woman there to be my son's wife.*'
> GENESIS 24:7 (NEW LIVING TRANSLATION)

Are you feeling lonely or lost on your journey? Are you looking for that special someone? Maybe you are with someone and you need a little extra help.

Angels can't make someone fall in love with you. They don't manipulate the free will of another person but they can help you to feel good about yourself. Finding peace with yourself is the first step towards finding love in your life. Sometimes that love comes in the form of romance and other times it appears as loving friendships.

Communication is often the key to romance and Archangel Gabriel is the angel to call upon in that situation. Archangel Ariel assists with unresolved problems but the most important archangel would be Haniel who helps with romantic love and relationships.

> 'We are never so lost our angels cannot find us.'
>
> **STEPHANIE POWERS**

Personal and spiritual development

Are you ready to explore your inner self? Have you suddenly become aware that life is not all it seems? Do you know that you have the ability to direct and control the largest part of your life journey – or at least think you do? Then you are ready to ask your angels for their help.

Angels can make many suggestions for ways in which you can explore your spiritual self. This knowledge comes to you as gut instinct and intuition. Follow your feelings and use this to guide your path. Your angels will help you to find things to try. Are you interested in learning a spiritual healing method? Do you want to learn meditation? Do you want to help others or learn about a new religion or spiritual practice? Try some of the many ideas which come your way – follow your own instincts.

Archangels Metatron and Sandalphon can assist you with your spiritual development. Ask them in your head or write down your request if you prefer. Archangel Zadkiel can assist your confidence in following your dreams. Ask Archangel Jeremiel to help you work on your psychic development.

> *'I have learned that if one advances confidently in the direction of his dreams, and endeavours to live the life he has imagined, he will meet with a success unexpected in common hours.'*
>
> HENRY DAVID THOREAU

Health and healing

Are you struggling with personal health issues? Do you fight with dieting or fitness problems? Do you suffer from long-term illness or everyday aches and pains?

There are several angels with the traditional role of healing and health and they are waiting for your request. Some health issues are related to other life problems and may involve greater degrees of investigation. Perhaps your backache is related to a stressful work issue, or maybe your 'pain in the neck' is related to a difficult person in your life! Not all things are what they seem!

Archangel Raphael is the leader of the angel healers. He can help with things such as operations and general doctor's appointments, and you can even ask Raphael to come with you to the dentist or optician. Archangel Uriel works with earth healing and Archangel Ariel heals animals and birds. Another archangel who is associated with healing is Sariel (although some reference him as a fallen angel!). As with all the suggestions here, if you feel that a different angel energy is working with you then go with that feeling.

> *'He shall give his angels charge over thee to keep*
> *thee in all thy ways.'*
>
> **PSALMS 9:11**

General life problems

Do you have problems with studying, planning, gardening? Do you need help with buying a new wardrobe or choosing a book to read?

There are angels for every task and role. Remember that you can also ask your own guardian angels to assist you with your day-to-day tasks. (There are many different lists of angels and their designated tasks are listed in my book *An Angel Treasury*.)

Archangel Chamuel helps to find lost objects and is concerned with human happiness. Gabriel helps with any number of writing tasks or difficult phone calls you might have to make and Archangel Michael is brilliant at mending broken objects. Sandalphon sends human prayers to heaven and Sariel is a teacher of knowledge, so there are plenty of angelic assistants to help with most challenges you might come across!

Annie told me about her angel experiences.

ANGELS FOR ... EVERYTHING

'A couple of weeks ago I was going through a horrible time, worrying about my exams, friendship problems and trying to deal with various experiences from my past. I had already started reading your book entitled An Angel Treasury, so I just started praying to the Archangel Gabriel out loud, asking him to help me get through my troubles.

My bedroom light flickered for a couple of seconds and the next morning I found a white feather underneath my desk which I felt had been left by the angels.

One of my problems was my poor circulation, so previously I always felt very cold. Suddenly, after asking for Gabriel's help, I felt very warm and became aware of love radiating within me. At the same time I became aware of the smell of lavender filling the room.

> *I've started praying to the angels when I'm having problems or feeling exhausted, and I can definitely feel their presence inside me. I have a tendency to let things cloud my mind and can get very stressed at times but after I have prayed (usually to the archangel Gabriel), I feel calm and serene and free of any negative feelings. I know I am being looked after by the angels.'*

Annie is not alone in noticing the scent of flowers when an angel is around – many people report lovely smells! Roses, gardenias and vanilla are some of the more common, although someone once woke up to the smell of fish and chips, which sounds more like a spiritual joke to me! The lady did suggest that it might be her father-in-law visiting from the other side as he was a big fish and chip fan! Tobacco and other unusual smells are normally provided as a 'reminder' by our loved ones in the after-life, rather than by your angel smoking a pipe! Scent is a power-ful way of receiving communication from spirit.

Angels are pretty good at manipulating things like electricity too. I often get flickering lights when my angels and guides are around me. Elaine shared her story.

LET THERE BE LIGHT

One night Elaine woke in the early hours of the morning and 'knew' instinctively that something wasn't right. She realized the landing light she leaves on for the children wasn't on, and then realized that in fact the electricity wasn't on at all.

After stumbling downstairs Elaine could see the whole street was out, so searched around for a torch. She decided to ring the electricity board on her mobile and was annoyed when they told her it would be another four hours before the electricity supply would be restored, and they were already sending electricians out to work on the problem.

Elaine decided to go back to bed and tossed and turned whilst she began to worry about the freezer and other electrical equipment. She couldn't remember which lights she'd tried to switch on and was concerned that the whole house would be lit up like a Christmas tree once the electric was restored!

Elaine thought it was time to call in her celestial back up and spoke to them in her head. 'Okay angels, if you really are there and want me to stop doubting both you and myself, restore the electricity in less than five minutes please.'

It was a real test but one the angels were happy to pass. Elaine says that in less than three minutes the electricity returned to normal and she was totally stunned. She said, 'I can tell you in all honesty that I nearly fell out of bed in shock! Once again the angels have given me proof they exist!'

Elaine's story might not seem like a miracle to most people but it's just one more piece in the puzzle. Do you have stories like this in your own life? We have to ask ourselves, 'Is this always a coincidence?' Angels like to help whenever they can but they also in turn ask us to assist them.

Ideas for ways in which you can help your angels

'We are each of us an angel with only one wing.
To fly we need only to embrace each other.'
LUCIANO DE CRESCENT

Angels regularly make use of human beings to send messages and bring assistance to other human beings. At the end of it all, when everything is done and dusted, the only thing that matters at all is the fact that we cared, that we loved and that we made a difference in someone's life. We can help our angels to help others.

Does it matter more that we give thousands of pounds to charity or that we smile at a stranger on the bus? Is it more important to buy a lotto ticket or help dig a well? Will you look back on your life and say, 'I did my best, I'm proud I made a difference.'

Of course, finding ways to make a difference in the world is very much a personal thing. We need to use our own natural talents and go where we feel drawn. A lot of the things we do to help people occur on the spur of the moment. You see a need and you fill it. We can all do this in many, many ways every single day of our lives. Small things make a big difference.

Start making a difference today.

> '*No other virtue makes man more equal to the angels,*
> *than the initiation of their way of life.*'
> JOHN CASSIAN

Little ways to make a difference. How to be an 'angel':

- ♥ Plant spring bulbs on waste ground.
- ♥ Feed the birds.
- ♥ Pay someone else's bill.
- ♥ Smile at strangers – smile at everyone!
- ♥ Pick up litter.
- ♥ Bake double quantities and give half away.
- ♥ Pay a compliment.
- ♥ Say thank you.
- ♥ Mow your neighbours' lawn when they are away on holiday.

'We can all be angels to one another. We can choose
to obey the still small stirring within, the little whisper
that says, "Go. Ask. Reach out. Be an answer
to someone's plea."'

JOAN WESTER ANDERSON

This is just a taster of the things you can do. Make a list of your own. Keep your acts a secret between you and the angels. There isn't a nicer secret you can keep!

connecting with yourself

'There is, therefore, a more perfect intellectual life in the angels. In them the intellect does not proceed to self-knowledge from anything exterior, but knows itself through itself.'

SAINT THOMAS AQUINAS

How can you know yourself?

How many of us really know who we are? We associate ourselves with our job, maybe our marital status or perhaps with how many children we have or where we live. 'I'm a Civil Servant,' we say, or, 'My name is Mrs so and so and I live in Devon,' or maybe, 'I'm Jill's husband.' What do we really want to say? What do we know about the inner us? How can we describe who we are inside? Most of us actually have no idea! We only see ourselves as connected with other people or life situations.

Could you say, 'My name is Sam and I am a special person with a caring personality. I am kind and generous and spend time listening to people when they are in need.'

No? Why not? In our western society, to express our personal attributes and to be proud of them is in some way seen as wrong.

But you can be proud of your achievements and be humbled by them at the same time. Always acknowledge your successes - even if it's only to yourself.

Have you ever met YOU? Angels know the inner us, our real and genuine selves. They do not judge or criticize us in any way. They love us for exactly who we are right now. Do you love yourself? This is one of life's biggest challenges; to know and to love yourself.

Looking in the mirror

Go and stand in front of a full-length mirror right now.

- ♥ Try not to feel embarrassed. Say 'hello' to yourself.
- ♥ Smile. Try not to giggle!
- ♥ Look into your own eyes and say, 'I love you.'

Do you find that hard? Most people would. Do you feel silly? Does it feel 'big headed' to love yourself?

I want you to practise saying to yourself, 'I love who I am right now,' and other positive phrases. Look into your own eyes in the mirror as you say this. Face yourself.

- ♥ Say, 'I am proud of the way I handled that difficult situation at work.'
- ♥ Say, 'My garden looks beautiful, I worked hard on it.'

♥ Say, 'I pleased Emma when I spent time with her today. I did well.'

Celebrate your successes. Congratulate yourself when you do well. It's funny how easy we find it to make criticisms of our behaviour, but not the other way round. Most of the time, we do the best we can, and that's all we can do. Our life is a learning situation and we move forward and grow as spiritual beings from every encounter.

Remember – there is not always a right or wrong way to do a task, just the way we choose. Life does not always fit into perfect boxes. We weigh up all the options and make a choice, or not. That's life. Be less harsh on yourself. To love yourself is to feel the spiritual nature of your being, to be connected to the universal energy, the energy of pure love (bliss).

Ask your angels to help you to face yourself. Ask them to help you love yourself in the way they love you: unconditionally.

In time and maybe through very many life incarnations, the question, 'Who am I?' changes to simply, 'I am.'

Who am I?

To find out who you are, you need either a large sheet of paper and a pen or a friend to ask the questions.

FRIEND VERSION

Set up a tape recorder (so you have a record of your answers, if you wish) and get your friend to sit opposite you. Your friend will ask you the question, 'Who are you?' You must answer the question immediately. Then your friend asks again, 'Who are you?' and so on. This could result in your friend asking you the same question 50 times or more until you feel you have no more answers.

Everyone starts off the same way, by giving their name, 'I am Mary.' You might then follow the pattern and then share your immediate family connections, 'I am Leo's Dad,' 'I work at the supermarket,' and so on, followed probably by the car you drive and your hobbies. The interesting bit starts when you get down to answering the question for the twentieth time!

So, who are you? Hopefully by the time you get to the end of this exercise, you will know a little more about who you are. You might be surprised at your answers!

WORKING ALONE

If you don't have someone you can work with, then you can write down your answers. Write down the words, 'Who am I?' at the top of the page and then write your answers, leaving a line between each answer (to create a list rather than sentences which are not so clear to analyse afterwards).

After each answer you write down, ask yourself the question again in your head or out loud. You could also ask the questions yourself and then speak the answer into a recorder if you prefer. See how you do. You will probably learn something about yourself that you were not immediately aware of.

Preparing yourself for a clearer channel

Recently I have felt very drawn to detoxing my body. 'Detoxing' is a very over-used word at the moment but we do clog up our bodies with too much fat and sugar, amongst other things. Spirit finds it more difficult to work with a body which is weighed down with modern-day toxins. Fumes from factories, cars and cigarettes, as well as caffeine, alcohol and drugs, are all poisons to the system. Imagine trying to talk to your angels through a closed door!

My own angels have led me to try different clearing and cleansing programmes. With my own free will I have decided on the things which I can live with and those I cannot! I have tried to adjust my diet so that I am eating more healthily. My own angels did not say to me, 'Stop drinking alcohol,' or 'Don't eat chocolate,' but they did say, 'Eat good food.' How I went about that was up to me.

When I asked the angels why I was undergoing this physical change in my dietary habits they simply replied, 'To make yourself a clearer channel for the angels.' They can literally contact me more easily if I take better care of myself. And what a great pay off! Eating less chocolate means thinner thighs, and less weight on my body means I move more easily and I am being kinder on my heart. You don't have to give up everything, just think more carefully about what you put in your body. Decide, 'Will eating this help my body or my mind?'

Actually, sometimes that chocolate biscuit is exactly what you need, but do try to stay in the moment. Always stop what you are doing and appreciate the food that you are eating. So many people read, watch TV or do something else at the same time as eating, and we have no idea WHAT we are putting in our mouths! Make sure that slab of raspberry cheesecake is actually lifting your soul. It is? Then go ahead and enjoy!

Bodily cleansing

It might sound silly to mention it but regular cleansing of your outer body is as important as cleansing and detoxing the inside. Toxins (often city grime) can build up in our clothes, skin and hair. Harsh chemical cleaning products are very much a way of life nowadays. Maybe you could try some gentler alternatives?

Some people recommend bathing in sea salt baths before commencing any spiritual communication (salt is a traditional cleansing tool). Maybe this will work for you? Water is also a great way of communicating with the angels. So many people feel their angels around them when their body is immersed in water. I can't think of a better 'excuse' to luxuriate in a warm bubble bath!

The 'miracle' drink

I have recently discovered a wonderful drink. This miracle drink makes me feel fantastic. What is this wonder you may ask? Hot water! What? Yes, I really said hot water!

Most of us need to drink more water every day. I always found it hard to swallow large quantities of cold water so this is perfect for me. The first cups tasted strange, like the weakest tea I had ever had, but by cup four I had actually started to request warm water as my daily beverage of choice. Actually, the hardest thing about drinking warm water is that people look at you as if you are crazy! People around you will get used to it but initially they will ask, 'Do you want a teabag in that?' Um, no thank you!

Drink it hot or cold but just drink it!

Exercise

Exercise? Oh how I hate that word. It always conjures up images of dragging behind at cross country running during high school games lessons. Do you like going to the gym? If you do, then good for you, but it's not for everyone. Find things that you enjoy … walking the dog, salsa dancing or skipping. A fit body is a clearer channel for the angels too.

Meditation

I used to feel sorry for people who meditated. What are all those people doing sitting crossed legged? How boring that must be? In my ignorance I had no idea. Meditation is a profoundly spiritual experience. Meditation can ease stress, open up your mind and make you more psychic. Yes, indeed, and now I do it too.

Regular meditation sessions are important, and again find what works for you. There are lots of different 'disciplines' which each involve their own techniques. You can chant whilst you meditate, listen to music, or concentrate on a single word, phrase or idea. Some methods involve clearing your mind completely and others involve following a journey through spoken word. I have created some 'guided meditation' CDs myself, and many people find these very useful (check out my website: www.JackyNewcomb.co.uk for more information.) You can also read and then remember 'a journey' to a spiritual destination, or create a special garden or beach area in your mind which you can return to over and over.

Don't have time to meditate? Find the time. It's the best ten minutes you can spend every day! Commune with yourself, commune with your angels and ultimately with your creator. Meditation is our way of listening to God in the way that prayer is the way we talk to 'him'.

Meditation is a sacred rite, so for goodness sake, allow yourself the privilege of closing the door behind you. I know this is not easy if you have children. Get into the habit of warning everyone before you meditate. Let them know that you will be unavailable to them for ten to twenty minute (unless the sky falls in). Stick a poster on your door saying, 'I am not here right now – ask people to ring back!' It works eventually!

With very young children, obviously make sure that they are not alone when you do this. Try sticking a picture on the door which indicates to them what you are doing. Let them actually 'see' you meditating (explain that it is a little like having a nap), and maybe get a photograph taken of you meditating and stick THAT on the door. I know this all sounds very 'over the top' but these things do work. Find ways to enable you to do the things you need to do in your life – meditation and otherwise.

All of these things are very 'ideal world', so don't stress yourself out if you are not eating the perfect food every day or can't exercise as much as you should. Becoming stressed about what you don't do is not the idea. We are human beings after all, not machines, so just do your best and be happy with that.

Grounding

Keeping in touch with real life is important too. We live in a real three-dimensional world. After meditating or communicating with your angels, bring yourself back into the here and now.

Some people can feel 'floaty' and disconnected for a while after meditating. This is not useful if you are just about to drive to work!

Ways to ground yourself:

- ♥ Drink a cup of tea.
- ♥ Eat something – the perfect time for that chocolate biscuit?
- ♥ Take your shoes off and walk outside.
- ♥ Hold a black crystal (hematite, for example).
- ♥ Sit in a chair and imagine you are a tree (stay with me here …). See yourself as having strong roots which go deep into the ground.

Make grounding part of your spiritual and meditation work. Ask your angels to help keep you grounded!

HUG A TREE MEDITATION
(Don't knock it till you try it!)

First find a quiet place to sit comfortably. Close the door behind you and stick your 'busy' sign on it if you share your home with others. Make sure the room is warm enough and that the phone is off the hook. There is nothing more annoying than being brought out of a deep meditative state by the ringing of a phone! Of course, in time and with practice these things will not disturb you.

If you intend to play background music whilst you meditate then choose something gentle without vocals which can be distracting.

Sit in a comfortable high-backed chair if you can. Or lie down if you are sure you won't fall asleep. Place your feet on the ground. Place a cushion under your feet if you have short legs like me!

Take two or three deep breaths, breathing in through your nose and out through your mouth. In and out … in and out … blowing the breath out through your mouth.

Breathe normally now, and imagine yourself standing in front of a tall, old tree. Walk up to the tree and ask permission to re-energize. When you hear the answer yes, place your arms around the trunk.

Imagine, now, the tree flooding your body with grounding energy. Feel the energy actually enter the top of your head and flood down through your body and into the ground. Spend as long as you need doing this.

Ask your guardian angel to pass on any words of wisdom

which you need for the coming day while this is happening.

When you are ready, come back into the room. You should feel grounded and refreshed already, but if you need to, follow one of the grounding tips suggested as well.

Of course you can actually do this with a real tree too.

'ALIGNING YOURSELF' MEDITATION

Follow the tips at the beginning of the previous meditation. When you are ready, begin.

Sit in a comfortable high-backed chair if you can. Or lie down if you are sure you won't fall asleep. Place your feet on the ground. Place a cushion under your feet if you need to.

Take two or three deep breaths, breathing in through your nose and out through your mouth. In and out ... in and out ... blowing the breath out through your mouth.

Breathe normally now and imagine yourself holding a staff (or walking stick) in front of you. The staff is the same height as your body but has coloured lights down it. Look at each of the lights in turn. Right at the top of the stick is a clear light, a little way down is a purple light, next is a blue light and then a green light. About a third of the way down is a yellow light, followed by amber and finally, about half way a red light.

Look at each of the colours. They should all be glowing brightly. Are any of the colours duller than the rest?

Concentrate on each colour in turn. Using the power of your imagination, turn up the brightness so that each colour is glowing and healthy looking. Balance each of the colours using your imagination.

See them now, starting at the top and working your way down. Check:

- ♥ Clear
- ♥ Purple
- ♥ Blue
- ♥ Green
- ♥ Yellow
- ♥ Amber
- ♥ Red

Bring each colour into line. Keep checking up and down to see if the colours are all the same and 'boost' some energy into any which need attention, using the power of your mind.

Each colour represents an 'energy centre' and corresponds with the colours most people recognize as their

> 'chakra' colours (chakra is a Sanskrit word for wheel).
>
> *When you are ready, slowly bring yourself back into the room. Follow one of the grounding methods if necessary.*

You can do this exercise any time you are feeling 'off balance'.

8
angel workshops— and learning more

Each journey begins with the first step …

Are you ready to learn more? This book is just the beginning of your journey and you can have a lot of fun creating a personal relationship with your own angels.

What's an angel workshop?

If you are interested in learning more about angels, why not attend an angel workshop? Workshops are places where like-minded people can get together and learn more about angels. Each angel workshop is going to be different depending on the angel teacher – and students attending, but some of the subjects you might cover include:

Sharing angel stories

One of the most exciting things about attending an angel workshop is to be able to talk about the magical things that have happened to you and listen to other people's angel experiences. Many say to me, 'This is the first time I have been able to share my own experience with people who really understand!'

When I run an angel experience I always feel I learn as much from my students as they do from me. I love to hear other people's angel stories. We all do.

Using angel divination cards

There are numerous angel divination cards available to buy. These simple cards with positive and loving words and phrases are very popular now. Even children can use them safely. Some workshops will teach you how to use them (fairly easy to do) or even show you how to make your own cards at home. I have covered this subject in greater detail in my book *An Angel Treasury*.

Joining in group meditations to meet your guardian angel

Meeting your guardian angel in a meditation with a group might be easier for you than trying to do this alone. Some people feel apprehensive or overawed at what might happen to them. Being with other people when you do this for the first time can make you feel more comfortable. Sharing your experiences afterwards is also part of the fun.

Everyone's experiences with this sort of exercise vary greatly. For people who have never meditated before, the meditation might be little more than 'a relaxing experience', but others who have meditated before, even just two or three times, may benefit more.

Some people are moved to tears by the feelings of unconditional love that they receive from their guardian angel when they meet for the first time. Experienced teachers always have a box of tissues handy just in case!

I've also had occasions when a deceased loved one pops into the meditation with a loving message or words of comfort, and although our loved ones are not angels as such, they can look after us in a similar way.

Chanting and drumming

Chanting and drumming are fun ways of getting the energy moving in the room! Some teachers use native drumming as a way of bringing people into a meditative state, ready for meditation work.

Energy work

Bring in columns of light to send out to troubled areas or to use for healing.

Visualizations are very powerful and, like joint prayer work, the more people working together on a common theme, the greater the power. Joining our thoughts together to create positive thoughts of peace and love to send to others who need it is one of the most beneficial parts of an angel workshop. Your angel teacher will show you how to do this.

Singing

Like chanting and drumming, singing can really lift the energy and lighten the soul! This can also be enormous fun (but perhaps not if you are a poor singer like me).

Space clearing

Many teachers use feng shui space clearing techniques in all of their angel work. I always clear and prepare a room before use, by smudging (a traditional Native American technique of burning dried sage in a room to clear negative energies), and infusing frankincense oil (I add a couple of drops of oil to water in the top of my oil burner) to raise the energy of the room which, in turn, assists angelic communication.

Other people use music, bells, drums, angel sprays and so on to clear the room. Ask your angel teacher for guidance.

Preparing sacred spaces

Apart from space clearing, you might learn about other ways of preparing the room for angel work. Your teacher might use crystals, candles, flowers and other natural products as well as other angel 'tools'.

Learning methods for 'tuning in' to your angels

There are so many ways of contacting and working with your angel and I learn new techniques all the time. My own angels often contact me in dreams (I show people ways of asking for answers to queries and questions before going to bed at night). My students use many creative methods of their own so I always try and leave time for people to share ideas with each other.

Learning your guardian angel's name

I often do this using meditations but your teacher may have other methods. 'How do I find out my guardian angel's name?' is probably the question I am asked more than anything else. For some people it is as simple as just asking for the name. The name may pop right into your head … if you ask!

Writing to your angels

Letters, notes, rituals and magic. Lots of different ideas fit into this category. You can learn how to write with your angels and ask them questions using a type of 'automatic writing'. Ask your question and immediately write down the first answer that comes into your head. Writing down your questions and queries can bring the request to life and give it more power!

Journalling with your angels

If you are serious about writing to your angels you might want to write with them on a daily basis. Your angel teacher will have many ideas on how to do this using a special notebook or journal. It's nice to burn a special candle while you do this and dedicate the candle to your angels.

Playing 'angel' music

Many people have created beautiful music based upon real angelic choir sounds that they have heard for themselves. A lot of classes play this type of music during the workshops.

This is just a small selection of the things you might do at an angel workshop. You can find angel teachers on the internet or perhaps look at some of the adverts in spiritual and holistic magazines. Contact a few and find out what they do. Good teachers will be happy to talk to you beforehand. I also run classes myself.

If you are lucky you will also be able to purchase books and other angel-related items at your workshop, which you can bring home to continue your study. Some teachers will provide a certificate to mark your day and they might make themselves available if you have questions or experiences you wish to discuss after the day has finished. Always check so that you understand what your class includes.

Class sizes vary greatly and I have given talks and workshops to between one and several hundred people. Do remember, though, larger classes will be very different to smaller groups. There will be less time (or no time) to ask questions and it will naturally be more difficult to create an intimate meditation experience with your angels!

Prices vary greatly but there is usually a good reason. Home workshops might well be cheaper than those at expensive venues. Is food included in your day? Does your teacher have to travel a long way or stay in hotels? All these things will have to be taken into consideration. Workshops take a great deal of preparation and your teacher may have spent a lot of time and effort creating worksheets and other materials. Find out if you will need to bring anything else with you, though, just in case.

Will you need to travel? Perhaps you can share expenses with several friends. It's nice to be able to discuss your day together afterwards.

Working in a group — getting started

Find out if there are people in your local area who share your interests. Perhaps you could place a postcard or a small poster in a local 'new age' shop, or a discreet card in a newsagent's window. The shop owner might even be able to help you and may already know locals who are interested in setting up a group. Check out any business cards that they might have at the front of the shop. Local psychics who give 'angel card' readings and similar might be useful contacts. See if other development groups are advertising in your area — maybe there is already a group that you can join which is already set up and running.

Other sources of inspiration are local mind, body and spirit fairs and advertisements in popular holistic magazines. Do your research first!

Also ask around your immediate friends and colleagues. You will be amazed how many people will actually say, 'I had no idea you were interested in angels, too!'

Next, you need to find a suitable meeting space. If you decide to hold your angel group at your own home you will want to make sure that you are happy about who you are inviting! Decide if you want to charge a small fee to cover the cost of tea and coffee, etc. Fix a regular day or date for your get-togethers. If you agree a few dates in one go (and maybe get them printed off as handouts), then it will help to keep the group interest.

Think about themes for your group. It will be fun to cover different topics each session. Perhaps you could discuss ideas when you first get together?

Here are some other things you might like to try:

♥ Start an angel book lending library with your group. Keep proper records of who has which book and agree a deadline for when books have to be returned. Make a formal system by signing the books in and out; that way there won't be any disagreements over where the books have gone! Perhaps you could charge a small fee for each week a book is borrowed, which could go to a favourite charity.

♥ Use different types of angel divination cards and give each other readings. Learn to use the cards without the book, using your instincts alone.

♥ Take it in turns to run a different section of the meeting. Each person in turn can bring along any necessary tools.

♥ Learn about the different angels and what jobs they do. Perhaps you could concentrate on a different angel each time (see my book *An Angel Treasury* for a comprehensive listing). Have fun quizzes to test your knowledge.

♥ Find out on the internet or in holistic magazines and psychic newspapers about healing requests around the world. Work together with others, using the power of collective thought and the help of your angels to send healing around the world where it is needed.

- ♥ Read meditations from books (take it in turn), or consider making your own meditation recordings. New age stores also sell guided meditation CDs you might like to try as a group – you can also obtain them over the internet or by mail order.

- ♥ Create 'wish lists' of things you would like your guardian angels to help you with (work issues, home life, personal development, and so on).

- ♥ Share creative work that you have done. Have you been inspired by angels to create beautiful artwork or poetry, for example? Share with the group how you have done this.

Working alone

If you prefer to work alone then you can still do lots of different things.

- ♥ A quick search on the internet will bring up thousands of different guardian angel websites. You might enjoy communicating with other people online or join chat groups. Many people post their personal angel stories on the internet for others to read and enjoy. I had little experience of using computers until I made this discovery several years ago and now you can't keep me off the computer!

- ♥ Create your own angel website – it's fairly easy to learn, and don't be put off if you have no experience. Try a free website to get you started.

- ♥ Hundreds of books have been written about angels. Ask your angels to help you to find the books which are right for you. Sometimes books literally fall off the bookshelf as you walk by!

♥ You can easily play meditation tapes by yourself (and might well have more success at working quietly alone). Make notes about your experiences.

Let the angels inspire you!

ANGELS

The aim of the *Angels* DVD is to produce a refreshing and uplifting film that not only presents interesting information about the world of angels but essentially creates a comforting, assuring, and positive feeling that the viewer will want to experience again and again. Presented by leading experts in the field of Angels – Jacky Newcomb and Shirley Crichton.

Angels is available from New World Music:
www.newworldmusic.com

AN ANGEL TREASURY

*A Celestial Collection of Inspirations,
Encounters and Heavenly Lore*

JACKY NEWCOMB 'THE ANGEL LADY'

An Angel Treasury is a truly unique combination of reference book and inspirational guide. Answering all your questions about the angelic realm, it also shows us how angels appear in people's lives to heal, assist and offer guidance. Both a comprehensive almanac and a life-affirming collection of quotes and stories about real encounters with these heavenly beings, this is a treasure trove of celestial inspiration.

Available now in paperback – ISBN 0-00-718954-0